YOUR DOG—Companion and Helper

I PITY THE MAN

I pity the man who has never known
The pleasure of owning a pup;
Who never has watched his funny ways
In the business of growing up.

I pity the man who enters his gate
Alone and unnoticed at night,
No dog to welcome him joyously home
With his frantic yelps of delight.

I pity the man who never receives,
In hours of bitterest woe,
Sympathy shown by a faithful dog
In a way only he seems to know.

I pity the man with a hatred of dogs;
He is missing from life something fine;
For the friendship between a man and his dog
Is a feeling almost divine.

Author Unknown

Photo by Peter Chew

Also by Milo D. and Margaret E. Pearsall:

The Pearsall Guide to SUCCESSFUL DOG TRAINING, Howell Book House, 1976, 1980

and by Milo Pearsall and Charles G. Leedham:

DOG OBEDIENCE TRAINING, Charles Scribners' Sons, 1958, 1979

YOUR DOG
Companion and Helper

by Milo D. Pearsall and Margaret E. Pearsall

1980
Alpine Press, Inc.
1901 South Garfield, Loveland, Colorado 80537

Library of Congress Cataloging in Publication Data

Pearsall, Milo D.
    Your dog, companion and helper.

    Includes index.
    1. Dogs—Training.   I. Pearsall, Margaret E.,
joint author.   II. Title.
SF431.P39   636.7'0887   80-14115
ISBN 0-931866-07-3

International Standard Book Number 0-931866-07-3
Library of Congress Catalog Card Number 80-14115

First edition—1980.
Printed in the United States of America.
Second Printing—1982

DEDICATION

To the many who, over numerous years, have brought their training problems to us, furnishing the challenges that resulted in adding to our ability to counsel, advise, and come up with solutions for them and their canine companions.

Margaret & Milo

FOREWORD

"Hey, you, with the Bulldog! How would you like me to put that chain and heavy leash on you and jerk?"

Who was this man, and why was he yelling at me? This was my first encounter with Milo Pearsall. Sound bad? Let me back up a bit. It was my first training seminar in Wisconsin in 1969, and I was a beginner. I had two bulldogs with me so I did stand out from the crowd a bit. Besides, I thought, "How do you train a bulldog? You have to be tough, right?"

Wrong! After Milo got my attention, he taught me that there were other ways to train dogs, even bulldogs. I have never forgotten that episode. Milo does not hesitate to yell at a young trainer, but his purpose is not one of humiliation; it is one of forcing the owner to ask himself if *he* would undergo the same procedure from the dog's point of view.

One of my dogs had her CDX, and the other was in progress toward her CDX. I could not force her to do anything, so at Milo's suggestion I put a small cotton collar and leash on the dog and began to work with her Milo's way. I talked to her, and carefully led her step-by-step, with tenderness and patience. I was learning to see things in the same way the dog sees things. And it worked! Together, we accomplished the near impossible—we attained the coveted title of Utility Dog. And on numerous occasions, people commented that she was one of the happiest working dogs they had ever seen. This happy ending was only the beginning.

At that first training seminar, Milo Pearsall planted a seed which became a reality for me in 1975. I entered an entirely new field—audio dogs for the deaf. We were brought together once again, Pearsalls and I, through our interest in this expanded use of "working" dogs. The Pearsalls have been involved with the utilization of dogs for the disabled for quite some time now and employ that same method of love, patience and viewing the problem from the dog's point of view. Milo has designed a bar to be placed on a wheel chair that keeps the dog at heel position for his handler. This is an example of the inspiration and reasoning Pearsalls display as they expand their expertise and experience in training dogs and pursuing new, innovative uses for the "working" dog. They are proving that "man's best friend" is that and much more.

I have had many talks with Milo and Margaret since starting the hearing dog program. All of our dogs come from shelters, and the most perplexing problems trainers oftentimes face is "What has happened to this dog before he came here and how is it going to affect his training?" For instance, one dog upon delivery to her new deaf master became hysterical when seeing carlights flashing at night. She also destroyed certain items in her owner's bedroom. Using Milo's method of getting down to the dog's level and seeing what the dog sees, we learned that the only articles destroyed were items that reflected light. We had found a pattern—she was afraid of reflected light. Once we knew the pattern, we could train the dog. I can list many examples of how dogs have been frightened by the television, electric fences and bicycles, to name a few. However, as a trainer, I could never have realized what the existing problem was without getting down to the dog's level, and since we have trained dogs as small as four pounds and as large as one hundred pounds it is important to view things from the *right* level.

I would, personally, like to thank Milo and that soft-spoken lady, Margaret, who gave me the confidence and inspiration to seek out and pursue a totally new field for dogs—training hearing dogs for the deaf—and for sharing their methods now in YOUR DOG, COMPANION AND HELPER. Through this book both normal and disabled trainers will learn to view training from the dog's point of view. And, for the first time, the book puts together for disabled trainers guidelines for training their own dog. It is also a valuable aid to trainers hoping to work with the disabled handler, and to dog owners and trainers everywhere who hope to understand their dog better.

Agnes McGrath
Hearing Dogs, Inc.

PREFACE

As many of our friends and acquaintances already know, during all but the first of our years in obedience training (when we were unaware that there was more than one way to train), we have made our prime goal that of teaching from the dog's point of view. We believe that the only effective and satisfactory way to teach anything to a canine companion is to approach it by trying to put one's self in his place and imagine what things are like through his eyes, showing understanding and creating a rapport that can be gained no other way, in direct contrast to other methods where results are gained only through force and dominance.

In this text we have also given special consideration to the personal desires and needs of individual dog owners and have encouraged them to do their own selection of information and advice as dictated by those desires and needs.

There are so many different variations of needs and individual preferences in this world that it would be impossible to write one book on training that would satisfy all. That is why we chose to write this one in the manner we have.

We have given each reader an option to choose what he wishes, to make his own decision. He makes up his own mind as to whether he wants a puppy or an adult dog, a male or a female, a purebred or a mixed breed, whether he prefers to work him at his left side or his right, and have given special help and advice to those who are handicapped. We have pointed out advantages and disadvantages in the above to help the reader make the necessary decisions before he starts his training.

We hope we have contributed help to those who need it and also to the instructors who are interested in being a part of giving that help to them.

TABLE OF CONTENTS

Chapter 1
PREPARING YOURSELF

On first thought, it might seem a bit ridiculous to bring up the idea of "preparing yourself" to become the owner of a puppy or a dog. But let us delve into some of the factors that could and should influence this step you may be contemplating.

Many benefits may be gained from the pleasures of owning a dog, but you need to be aware of the drawbacks as well. We do not want to discourage you in this move, but we do want to enlighten you so that you do not jump into a situation unaware of what is involved. A lack of understanding can lead to a change of heart later on, and the victim will be another unhappy, neglected, cast-out member of our canine world.

Our own experiences with dogs go back to our childhood days, long before we knew each other and long before we understood purebred dogs, dog shows, or dog registration. But we did learn about the love that develops between dogs and people, about the importance of caring for dogs and training them, and about their usefulness to mankind. We learned, too, how each dog differs in its own personality and characteristics, regardless of how great a pedigree it may have or whether it's a "Heinz 57" mixture. Each dog has a brain that you can help to develop and a heart with an endless capacity for love and loyalty. We hope to draw upon many of our own experiences, as well as those of other people, and pass on our observations and counsel to help you in your new role if you decide to get a dog for a pal.

Some Vital Considerations

To begin with, you want a healthy puppy or a well-cared for dog. Where he comes from may influence this factor and definitely deserves investigation. Don't be taken in by advertising from unreliable pet shops that often deal with "puppy mills" for their stock. If you're looking for a good buy and don't care whether or not the dog is purebred, visit your local pet shelters and consider adopting one of their residents. But do it with your eyes open! Good health is very important and your veterinarian should make this decision for you. Even if a friend wants to give you a pup, insist first that the puppy has a clean bill of health. Remember that you're investing in a pet that, hopefully, will be an important part of your family life for perhaps the next ten to fifteen years. You want to be sure that he gets a sound, healthy start.

Are You Ready for the Responsibility?

Now, let's examine your own motives. Are you considering getting a dog to please just one member of your family, or will the whole family become involved and will they be willing to share the responsibilities of owning and caring for the dog? Are you being selfish, thinking only of the pleasure that you alone expect to gain? If there are children in the family, are you capable of handling problems that might develop due to jealousy? Are there any members of your family who have physical problems that should be considered, or who just object to dogs or are afraid of them?

What about the reactions of your children's playmates? And do not forget your all-important neighbors! Can you assure them that your dog will be trained to be a good canine citizen, will be under control, will be friendly, and will be no threat to their property? Right now, *before* you bring either a grown dog or a young puppy home, is the time for you to find out what your neighbors think about another canine being added to the area. Talk it over with them; have some friendly chats. You might even find that you have nicer neighbors than you thought. Of course, you may find that some of your neighbors would feel better about the whole thing if you offered to fence your backyard, or at least part of it, for a dog run. Perhaps they, too, have dogs and you can find out if the dogs are well cared for, healthy, happy, obedient, and friendly. If there are female dogs in the neighborhood you may want to inquire how the owners handle the situation when she goes through the heat (oestrus) cycle. Do they keep her from becoming a disturbing element to the other dogs in the area? Are there unneutered male dogs running loose in the neighborhood? You should consider these factors when making up your mind as to which sex you want to own.

You should also become familiar with local laws governing dogs. Be sure to learn if your community has leash laws and, if it does, what restrictions are set forth by them. Find out about licensing, health requirements, and inoculations needed. Learn what might be considered a health hazard, a noise nuisance of barking, or other community problems caused by dogs.

Can you look at all these matters concerning your dog from his point of view, rather than just your own? Are you prepared to take on the responsibility of his care, protection, and training that will help him to develop into an important, lovable member of your family?

Fig. 1-1. Look for a puppy that is friendly and playful.

The Human Factor

Now let's study in greater depth some of the things we have only touched on so far, especially the various human factors that you should consider before assuming the responsibility of dog ownership.

First, let's consider the younger set—the children of the family, the neighborhood, and of visiting relatives and friends. We are all aware of children's tendencies to tease animals, sometimes to the point of cruelty. Naturally, they are not aware of the possible damaging results, especially where a young, sensitive puppy is concerned. You must be prepared to educate the children and make them realize that a puppy is important as an individual, and that he has rights as a creature on this earth, just as each child has rights. Children need to understand the importance of sharing in the responsibility for protecting and educating this animal.

If jealousy develops, be ready to offer some other hobby or diversionary interest for the one who feels neglected or left out. Plan a schedule that allows each child in the family to assume certain chores and responsibilities for taking care of your pet. Help them to experience the ever-present love and devotion that a dog will give when he receives attention, care, and affection.

In continuing your "pre-owner" investigation, are you aware of any family members who may be allergic to dog hair? Regardless of the breed or the questionable origins of a crossbred, a certain amount of shedding of dog hair is inevitable. You must expect this and be ready to cope with it.

Also make sure that none of your family members are afraid of dogs. If they are, and are willing to try to overcome that fear, be ready to cooperate and assist them because it is not an easy or speedy accomplishment. It is a known scientific fact that a body throws off a definite scent when fear is present, and this scent is very evident to dogs, precipitating sometimes undesirable behavior in them. (Refer to discussions on tracking in our other books for a clearer understanding of how a dog scents and why he reacts in certain ways. *See* Bibliography.)

How about any travel plans you may have? Will you be able to take your dog with you, or will you have to leave him with friends or relatives, or board him at a kennel? Do you know of a reliable kennel that will give him good care while he is there? Is it clean and comfortable? Does it have an adequate exercise area? Are the rates affordable? If you plan to travel with your dog, are you prepared to train him so that he can be depended upon to behave and not howl his heart out or damage property when left alone in your quarters?

Also give some thought to the extra "caution" training that will be necessary in case you have young children, infants, elderly, infirm, or handicapped persons in your household. Don't expect a puppy, or even a fully grown dog, to be able to adjust to strange new situations without your help and supervision. This means patience and understanding from *his* point of view. He will also have to learn to get along with other pets already in your home, such as cats, birds, gerbils, hamsters, etc. They also may need supervision until they get used to the dog's presence.

One very important person for you to think about when you're considering the well-being of your new four-footed friend, is your veterinarian. He or she should be regarded as your, as well as your dog's, friend. We can't stress enough the importance of this man or woman and the fact that they have so much to offer for the little amount they demand from us for their services. Veterinarians love the animals that they care for or they wouldn't have chosen careers in this field. They understand animals and have abilities comparable to pediatricians, who must diagnose without being told *where* the pain is or *why* there is abnormal behavior. They put in many years of hard study to reach their goal and we should appreciate them and take advantage of their knowledge and experience in helping us to keep our pets healthy.

What Kind of Home Can You Provide?

Where is your pal going to live? The size of the available area, as well as its location (city, suburb, country, etc.) should be influencing factors in choosing your dog. If the dog is still a puppy, consider what his probable size will be when he is full grown. Even the smallest dog needs a certain amount of exercise, and the larger the dog, the more important an adequate romping area becomes. It's easy to care for the needs of a little dog the size of a Pomeranian, even if you're living in a small apartment that has no yard. But how would you and your dog adjust if he were the size of a great Dane? Or if he were a dog that loved to range in the fields and hunt? Think twice! Of course, there are many sizes of dogs in between these extremes. If you do have a yard, plan some sort of fencing for your companion's protection, even if it's only a section large enough for a run where he can enjoy some freedom.

If your dog will be living outdoors most of the time, it's up to you to see that he has a shelter designed for your particular climate (see diagrams for ideas). Be sure that his bed area is large enough so that he won't be crowded and uncomfortable when he achieves his full growth. See that an insulating air space separates the floor of his bed and the ground or floor (e.g., in a kennel or in a corner of your garage) and that the bed is not located in a draft. If your dog is going to spend much time in the yard or in his run, see to it that his house is located in the shade. Let him be his own boss as to whether he wants to lie in the sun and for how long. He knows this better than we do.

If you and your dog have an unlimited living area, such as a farm, both of you can look forward to many extra hours of freedom and enjoyment. You'll have a much greater selection in choosing a dog to begin with, and you will be able to train him for special tasks around the farm. A working dog is always a much happier dog because he loves to please his owner by performing and doing something that is useful and appreciated. Farm dogs that herd and protect the farm population are always eager to work. They naturally prefer to stay close by their charges, living and sleeping in a barn, stable, or other comfortable outbuilding. Your dog can always "visit" you in the house if he wishes (and he'll find a way to let you know). He should be welcomed on these occasions provided you have done a good job of teaching him house manners and have kept him groomed and clean. He certainly merits that much attention and concern on your part.

If it's impossible for you to fence the yard or provide a run for your pet, but you still need to confine him, you can do this humanely by constructing an overhead cable from his comfortable doghouse to a designated point on a tree, post, or building. The cable should give him enough distance so that he can get proper exercise. Attach a lightweight chain from his plain buckled collar (*not* a slip collar that tightens up) to a sliding ring on the cable.

This will allow him freedom to travel back and forth as he wishes (*see* diagram).

If your dog is to reside inside your home, you will have to decide on some basic ground rules first. Will any rooms be off limits for him? And how about the furniture? Where will you plan his sleeping quarters and his feeding area? Will you allow him to be near you when you're dining, or will you teach him to remain in another area until you have finished? *A dog enjoys his life much more if he's been taught his restrictions and his privileges and if you're consistent with him once he has learned.*

In your residence, will you need to teach your dog to go up and down stairs or ride an elevator? Do you want him to be quiet when he's left alone; be unaffected by outside noises made by people, trains, airplanes, traffic, etc.? He may require some special attention, too, to get him used to riding in a car. This is especially important because you'll need to make trips to your veterinarian.

We've tried here to point out the pros and cons of dog owner-ship to help you decide if you want to assume such a responsibil-ity. If you do, you should strive to be a proud owner and be glad that you made the decision. You should be ready to meet any problems that might be involved, yet enjoy the enrichment that a

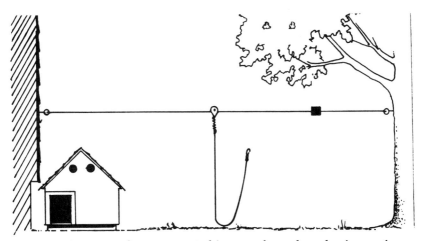

Fig. 1-2. A run can be constructed in an unfenced yard using a wire cable with a pulley block on the cable.

companion dog can give you. No reward can compare to the love and devotion that you receive from a canine pal. In addition, if you do a good job of training, you will gain immense satisfaction from the relationship that will have developed between you and your dog.

Now, go get that puppy or dog, and in the following pages we'll work with you step-by-step to help you develop him into the pal that you've dreamed of owning. The training will be fun for both of you. You'll become a team that will be a credit to your community. He'll love and protect you, will be loyal to you, and sympathetic, and will share your joys and sorrows. And he could care less whether your wallet is fat or thin as long as you are there.

Just remember to use your head, as well as your heart, when you choose him. He'll be yours, and you'll be his for the rest of his life!

Chapter 2
CHOOSING
THE RIGHT DOG

As we all know, man's tastes are as varied and far apart as the ends of the rainbow. We would be the last ones to contradict that statement, and we believe completely in the old adage, "What is one man's meat can be another man's poison." But regardless of personal preference, it's generally accepted that a certain amount of common sense and logic should come into play, regardless of the subject being discussed. Making snap decisions is always a risk. Therefore, before deciding what kind of dog you want, read these pages thoughtfully. We want to help you choose the right dog for you.

What About a Puppy?

A young puppy needs your time and attention. A schedule for feeding, watering, exercising (body eliminations), napping, playing, grooming, and kindergarten training must be established. Housebreaking alone is something to which you *must* devote time and attention, because a puppy's organs have not yet developed and matured to the point where they can "hold it." Most puppies want to be clean and will try to conform to your schedule if you're consistent and don't expect the impossible. But remember: if no one will be at home to take care of these details, a young puppy is not for you.

It is also necessary to give special attention to a young puppy who has just suffered the traumatic experience of separation from his mother and littermates and been brought into completely unfamiliar surroundings peopled with strangers and odd new sounds and smells. At this point he needs reassurance and understanding, without pampering and spoiling. Help give him an identity!

As a young puppy grows and becomes a part of your family unit, he naturally will depend on you for guidance and training, just as a child is trained and educated by his parents and teachers. So it is up to you to be alert and plan ahead to avoid the development of bad habits. If your puppy starts his life with you at about seven or eight weeks of age (the ideal age recommended by animal researchers), he hasn't had too much time to be taught any bad habits by his mother or littermates. Thus, you gain on this point because you can pretty well shape him along your own ideals.

Now let's look at the other side of the coin. If you're thinking of getting a fully grown dog, remember that he necessarily is already trained in many things, but is he trained the way you want for living with you? Are you going to have to work on *de*training first? Habit patterns have been established, some manmade, others not. If you want a housebroken dog on account of your own working pattern, can you be assured that you're getting one? Remember, too, that it is just as important to start out with a healthy adult dog as with a healthy puppy. Don't run the risk— have him checked.

Be sure you know what size accommodations are necessary so that you can make these preparations for him. At least there will be no guesswork as to how big a bed he'll need "when he grows up." And he will have done his teething on some bones or toys or somebody else's shoes and furniture. What is his temperament like, and how sure can you be of it? Do you have any way of checking his past environment? Do you know if he's had any bad experiences that have influenced him and may cause behavioral problems? Is this dog accustomed to meeting strangers, adjusting to new noises and locations, and accepting children? Remember that it takes time and much understanding and patience to remake unwanted habits in an older dog, but it *can be done* if you're willing to take it easy.

Disposition

If at all possible, check the disposition and personality of the dog's parents (this is not always easy to do if you are getting a grown dog). However, if this cannot be done, look for an alert, friendly, and naturally curious character—an extrovert that is independent yet loves people. Beware of the one that is shy, timid, and nervous and that barks and runs away from you, or the one that is too quiet or too aggressive. Look for a dog that responds well to a pleasant tone of voice and one that enjoys bodily contact, such as being petted.

Sex

You also must decide if you want a male or a female. If you choose a male, should you have him altered? Or will you be able to control him under all conditions if he's not?

If you decide on a female, will you be ready to protect her twice a year, about three weeks each time (on the average), so that she won't be producing unwanted, give-away puppies? Too many unwanted pets are already running the streets, filling the pet shelters, or having to be boarded and/or put to sleep, using tax dollars needlessly. Can you afford to have your dog spayed?

If you plan to get a purebred female, is it because you want to try your expertise at breeding? Are you interested in show competition, in field trials, or in working trials? If so, take advantage of the information and advice that is available from the American Kennel Club, 51 Madison Avenue, New York, New York 10010.

If you want a female for the prime purpose of educating the children about the facts of life, please think twice! This is being *most* unfair and is one of the greatest factors contributing to the serious national problem of pet population explosion. Whether purebred or mixed breed, there are already too many puppies and dogs being euthanized because they have no homes, no people who want them or will care for them.

A female dog generally has one excellent characteristic that may favor choosing her rather than her male counterpart. Usually females are much more content to stay at home. Many males are wanderers, especially if they get the message that a neighborhood girlfriend would like to have them pay her a visit! It's unbelievable what a male dog can do, going under, over, or through fences or other barricades, out windows, or even through screen doors, just to arrive at that certain destination.

Feeding

Regardless of your dog's age, be prepared to continue the feeding schedule to which he is accustomed, heeding the time schedule as well as the food. If you want to make any changes, make them very gradually. Many dogs' systems are sensitive to such changes, and you want to avoid unnecessary upsets during the adjustment period. Common sense and forethought can forestall an emergency trip to the veterinarian.

Grooming

Coat care should be considered from your own viewpoint. How much time and effort should you spend to keep your dog's coat looking fine and in good condition? Are you willing to devote that much to it, week after week? How much shedding is likely to occur? Will this bother you? Will it be too much for you to take care of? What type of coat do you prefer—short, long, curly, flat, or wavy? What color do you like—light, dark, parti-colored, or mottled? This is especially important if you want to hunt and need a dog that can be seen at a distance.

What about the grooming needed to keep the dog in good condition? This is as important as keeping your own hair healthy and clean. And you can't substitute false hair on a dog as no one makes wigs for dogs.

Along this same line, your dog's feet and toenails need attention. If the nails are not worn down by natural activity and exercise, they must be filed or clipped, and the hair must be cut between the toes to keep the pads of the feet in good condition. The ears should also be kept clean, and the eyes should be checked periodically by your veterinarian.

Health

The subject of health has already been mentioned, but we cannot stress this enough. Getting a healthy puppy or dog is a good start, but keeping him healthy is even more important. You must always be alert to the signs that may indicate abnormalities that should be checked by your vet.

Some things to watch for:

- teeth and mouth (discoloration, foul odor, broken teeth, bleeding gums, difficulty in chewing or swallowing)
- ears (carriage, sensitive to touch, shaking of head, foul odor, discoloration of hair inside, head carried to one side)
- eyes (any clouding or discharge, sluggish response to any movement)
- coat (beware of dull, sparse, and unusual shedding or indication of abnormal internal conditions)
- gait (should be free and easy; check irregularity in action, stilted, unnatural movement, favoring one leg)

Overall Assessment

Your next step is to weigh the qualities of a prospective puppy or older dog to see how they fulfill your own standard of performance.

Fig. 2-1. **Every age has its advantages and disadvantages.**

Are you looking for just a "lap dog companion"? Are you planning to use your dog for hunting? Do you want him to be a useful pal that will help you around your home or at work, or that will entertain you? Are you handicapped in any way and looking for a dog that will be an aid, as well as a companion? Do you want a dog for protection?

Depending on your dog's ultimate place in your living scheme, decide on the importance of temperament, size at maturity, personality, and previous environment, because all of these factors will affect the achievement, or lack of it, in reaching the goal that you have set.

The uses that you plan for your dog will have some bearing on whether or not you select a purebred. Naturally, if you want a dog that can be your companion but that can also be bred or can compete in AKC conformation or obedience shows, you will want

Fig. 2-2. All puppies are cute. Think about what you will expect from the grown dog before making your selection.

to choose a purebred, registered puppy. We suggest you research the various breeds that interest you carefully. Take plenty of time and visit as many breeders as possible before making your selection. If you are seeking a companion that can also work stock, pull a sled, or compete in field trials, learn something about each of the breeds that could perform these tasks, then make your selection after careful research. Find a breeder whose dogs are good in your chosen area of performance as well as friendly, even-dispositioned dogs that appear to make good companions.

Until recently only AKC registered dogs were eligible to compete for any kind of formal obedience degree. The United States All American Dog Obedience Guild, Inc., located in El Cajon, California, is attempting to change that situation. At present the organization is only active in California, but they hope to establish regional representatives in all parts of the country. All American participants earn obedience degrees in the same manner as dogs registered with AKC, except that they do not have to be purebred, registered animals. They must, however, be spayed, neutered, or have had a vasectomy to be eligible for USA DOGI obedience titles. The dogs participate in a practice obedience match at which a USA DOGI representative is present. They are judged as if they were at a formal trial and are awarded USA DOGI Certificates at three levels (novice, open, and utility) for qualifying scores at three matches. We think this is a great way to involve non-purebred dog owners in obedience training.

Now for the Search

You may need guidance concerning the best way to locate the dog that you want, so you'll be able to make a wise choice. Naturally, you're not likely to find mixed breeds in the same places as the purebreds, so let's take the purebreds first.

Purebreds can be obtained from a number of sources if you take a little time and put forth some effort. Refer to newspaper ads, local kennel and training clubs, the Yellow Pages, dog magazines, the American Society for the Prevention of Cruelty to Animals (ASPCA), and humane shelters, or write to the American Kennel Club. Sometimes you can find the dog you want in a local pet shop, especially if the shop has a good reputation, deals with recognized breeders, and runs a healthy, sanitary establishment.

Beware of the big franchised chains with the high-pressure fancy guarantees (*and* fancy prices) that will not tell you their source of supply. Most of them procure their stock from the big commercial puppy farms or "puppy mills," and their so-called "pedigrees" and registration forms aren't worth the paper on which they are written. The health of puppies from many of these establishments has also been questionable, in spite of statements and claims to the contrary. This has too often resulted in early death or permanent physical impairment to the innocent little creatures.

If you get a purebred puppy, it will be relatively easy to determine the characteristics of the mature dog, such as physical makeup, size, color, and general appearance, so this should not be a problem.

If your finances are limited, don't let this keep you away from a visit to a breeder, because you just might find exactly what you want. Many breeders sell their "pet stock" for reasonable prices, because they cull them from their breeding stock and possible show specimens. Most breeders welcome frankness from prospective customers when they realize that the customer doesn't want a pup for future breeding or showing and has limited finances.

Of course, the field widens if you would rather have a mixed breed of questionable parentage. Local clubs and newspaper ads are still good sources for leads, as well as the ASPCA and the humane shelters and animal adoption agencies. Usually the adoption fee is quite within reason and helps to defray supportive maintenance expenses. If you do plan to get a mixed breed, you *should* show enough sense to have it spayed or neutered so you won't be adding further to the unwanted over-population of the dog world.

Many times, through a neighbor, friend, or newspaper ad, you may be lucky enough to find a "giveaway" that suits your purpose. You also might run across some amusing reading in the classified section. One that we remember went something like this: "For sale, 8-week-old puppies, mother German Shepherd, father genuine Police Dog." Another that we saw was: "Puppies for sale, Laborador Retriever mother, Who Done It father." And speaking of mixed breeds, a current ad in our local paper offers "Doberdane puppies for sale."

You also should be aware of high-pressure advertising that extols the virtues of certain crossbreeds (accidental or purposeful). These dogs are *not* approved by any reliable organization and are not eligible for registration in the American Kennel Club. Some crossbreeds that a few people have been trying to promote are the Cock-a-Poo (Cocker Spaniel-Poodle), Peke-a-Poo (Pekingese-Poodle), Toy Boxer, Toy Shepherd, wolf-dog crosses, and others. Also being falsely promoted as rare breeds are some purebreds with disqualifying faults (as defined by the standards set up for those breeds), such as the White Shepherd, the White Boxer, and the Parti-colored Poodles.

In other words, do not believe everything that you read and hear on the subject. Learn to be resourceful and do some investigating on your own. Avoid snap decisions and think about the situation before reaching a verdict. Hopefully, your decision will lead to a satisfying, happy, and long-lasting relationship with a canine companion. Best of luck!

Photo by Deloris Reinke

Chapter 3
THE HOMECOMING

Advance Preparations

Before you can expect a happy and successful homecoming, you will need to make advance preparations that will help ensure your efforts to make this come true.

First, plan which room will be your dog's headquarters, so to speak (unless he is going to be an outdoor dog). Your best bet is usually the kitchen, or sometimes an enclosed sun porch. Most kitchen floors are easy to clean after accidents. And usually you spend quite a bit of time in that room, so it is easy to watch your dog's behavior and react as needed. You can also give the assurance and confidence required in this new situation. Kitchens usually have an easy exit to the outside, which is on the plus side for housebreaking.

Second, you should choose your equipment. We have found, as have many others with house dogs, that nothing is quite as efficient for giving dogs the security they need as the collapsible wire crate. It also serves as an excellent aid for housebreaking. The crate becomes the dog's bed, and he looks forward to using it to sleep in at night and for napping during the day. It is easily cleaned and can be equipped with a comfortable, washable pad, old towels or a piece of blanket. When he's in it, he can still see what is going on around him. We highly recommend this item. Be sure to get one that will be large enough for your new pal to lie down and stand up in comfortably, especially if you start with a small puppy. Try to estimate what his full size might be.

Other items that you will need include:

- Food and water dishes (easy to keep clean, difficult for your dog to tip over).

- A plain, buckled collar of flat or round leather or of a fabric such as woven or braided nylon.
- A short length of clothesline about one and one-half times the body length of the puppy. (*See* Chapter 4 for instructions on its use.) This is not important if you start with a mature dog.
- A leash (we often refer to it as a "lead"), about four to six feet in length, equipped with a small, lightweight snap that is easy to manipulate. The lead should be made of a narrow, strong fabric (such as webbing) or light leather and be easy on the hands. A chain lead is taboo, because it is noisy to the dog and can easily rip the hands of anyone using it to hold a dog, especially if the dog should make an unexpected lunge.

Fig. 3-1. **Training equipment you may need (clockwise from left):**
   whistles on lanyard
   web lead, spring snap
   white nylon lead, bolt snap
   narrow leather lead, spring snap
   web lead
   short "grab" lead, spring snap
   white web lead, squeeze spring snap
   plastic coated buckled puppy collar
   woven nylon buckled collar
   glove for teaching retrieving (in center)
   two sizes nylon training collars

- A blanket or pad for his bed in the crate and old towels for drying him after baths or dips; towels are also good for bedding because they are comfortable yet easy to launder.
- Toys—be careful and sensible in their selection. Bright-colored solid or sponge rubber balls are usually most attractive and come in several sizes that are small enough to be picked up and carried. Dogs and puppies also like treated bones, chewsticks, squeaky toys, bent-handle spoons, and toys made partially of latex. With a special box or container to hold all of his toys, such as an old shoe box, he'll soon learn that everything in that box is his personal property.

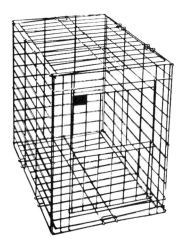

Fig. 3-2. A wire crate provides a safe, convenient "den" for your pet.

Fig. 3-3. Every house dog needs his own bed.

- Tie-out stake, for temporary use only at this time.
- Grooming equipment, such as brush, comb, nail clipper, file, small, rounded-point scissors, dog soap or shampoo, flea and tick spray, powder, or dip.
- Food—provided that you know in advance what kind your new dog will need. Otherwise, do some quick shopping on the way home so that you'll begin right. Be sure to read the labels thoroughly and keep a proper balance in your dog's diet.
- If you are planning to house your new friend outside your home, you may have to do some extra planning, build a house for him, and arrange for fencing a yard or run so that he won't be gallivanting around the neighborhood. There are endless ideas that have worked well for others and we've included some of them hoping to give you some help.

Fig. 3-4.   Tie-out stake. Can be moved for convenience.

Fig. 3-6.   A wire comb.

Fig. 3-5.   One of several types of brushes. This one is for smooth-coated breeds.

Fig. 3-7.   One type of nail clippers.

You may be so talented that you don't need any assistance, or you may want to alter the suggestions to better meet your specific needs. Whatever you decide, do your building and preparing before you leave to pick up the new dog.

Bringing Him Home

Now let's get down to the basics for the trip home. Be sure that you have newspapers or paper towels with you in case your dog has an accident. Remember: this ride could cause considerable tension and nervousness and perhaps an upset stomach. So be ready for anything and "play it cool." If an accident should happen, do not correct or punish the poor little guy for something that is beyond his physical control. Also, if possible, arrange for someone to drive your car for you on the way back or take you and bring you back. This will allow you to devote all your attention to the new family member. Be sure to bring the collar and leash.

When you arrive at your destination, find out from the breeder or former owner the feeding schedule to which the dog is accustomed. Ask how much the dog has been eating, how often, what brand names of food have been given, and when he last ate. (Hopefully his last meal was not too recent, since riding on a near-empty stomach is usually less disturbing than riding on a full one.) If you're taking home a purebred, be sure that all the required registration or ownership transfer forms are in order and are signed by the proper parties, ready for you to complete and send away.

Give the dog a chance to exercise and eliminate before putting him in the car. Make the experience as pleasant as possible, for this initial impression will carry right on through in his association with you. Your tone of voice, bodily contact as you lift and carry him, new noises of closing the car doors, starting the motor, vibration of the car, new smells, the sensation of motion, all contribute to the dog's impression. Reassure him, but do not baby him. This can be overdone and lead to undesirable behavioral problems.

From now on, your new friend will be learning from you, and you will be learning from him. Each of you will become increasingly sensitive to each other, aware of each other's needs and wants. You will learn to "read" him by his actions, his expressions, and any vocalizing that he may feel is necessary to get attention. He will learn from you, too, as he gets used to your voice, your movements, your special scent, and your touch. Use common sense as you introduce him to his new home and his bed, and let him explore his new yard. Allow him to relieve himself before reentering the house, then praise him profusely to let him know that he has done the right thing. Let him explore the yard for as long as he wants, to satisfy his curiosity. When back in the house, let him get acquainted with his bed and his quarters. Be sure that he's not penned up in an area that prevents him from seeing everything that is going on around him. See that newspapers are covering the floor well if housebreaking is high on your priority list.

House Training

Whether his first elimination is on the paper indoors or in a special area of the yard, be ready with a well-chosen word of praise, such as "Good!" and really draw it out and put a lot of happiness into your tone: "G-o-o-o-d!" When he is "in the act," use whatever command you would like him to associate with the action, such as "Hurry up," or "Find your place," then use the same words every time so that he'll know what you mean. He'll soon learn how much fun it is to please you and do what you want, as long as you express your pleasure.

If the first bowel elimination is unusually loose or runny, don't be unduly alarmed, because it may be caused by his nervousness and the sudden changes in his life. Give him time to return to normal. However, do check the stools for evidence of worms before disposing of them. Stools should not be allowed to remain in the yard, because they're a collection spot for flies and disease bacteria. Disinfect the area if possible, because an offensive odor may emanate from such deposits. If anything unusual shows, take your dog to the vet.

As you progress with housebreaking, try to encourage your pup to use the same area each time so that you can confine your pickup to as small a space as possible. Also, try to develop a

Fig. 3-8. Expansion gate placed across doorway to confine dog. Note assortment of toys to provide entertainment.

somewhat regular timetable for his outdoor excursions, dependent upon his own schedule of food and water intake, naps, physical play, night sleep, and other activities.

If the kitchen or sun room is being used for his new quarters, make provisions so that you can block any of the doorways and confine him to the one room. An expanding baby gate is a very effective piece of equipment. In fact, one company manufactures gates especially for dogs, and pet shops sell them. However, any substitute will suffice as long as it does the job for you.

Let your pup's introduction to his living quarters be as normal as possible. Reassure him with your voice when he needs it, but do not baby him. Encourage him to develop independence and do a little thinking on his own. Show him where his water is situated, but do not let him have enough to play in. When you first leave him alone by going out of the room, stay within his sight. If this is impossible, make your stay short so that your dog will not panic. After all, his mother and brothers and sisters are not there to keep him company anymore.

Establishing a Routine

It is very important for you to work out a schedule as soon as you know what will best satisfy both of you. You may have to juggle the schedule around a bit to accommodate his urges, but in the process you will learn to read your dog and respond to his needs. As he grows and adapts to his new home, he will change and will be able to extend the time interval between his trips to the "exercise" area outdoors. His body development will dictate these changes, along with encouragement by you in establishing his habits.

In addition to starting your puppy out on the diet and feeding schedule recommended by the seller, you'll need to consider future changes in it as he matures. Your best advice, of course, will come from your veterinarian. But the major dog food companies spend much money in research and experimentation so that they can sell you the best balanced food to satisfy total nutritional requirements of the average dog. Many also produce special food for puppies with extra body-building ingredients that growing puppies require. If your puppy or mature dog should need a special diet, your vet will advise you what to use.

When you start to feed your puppy a diet for a grown dog, be sure to make the change gradual, starting with a small amount of the new food mixed in at first and increasing the quantity week by week until the change has been made. You'll also notice that as the puppy grows he'll change his eating habits on his own, eating less than usual at a particular time of day. If he is on a three-meal timetable, he may first become less interested in the midday offering, then the breakfast meal, and may finally settle on just the evening meal. Sometimes a dog likes to have his main meal in the morning and a couple of biscuits in the evening.

We've found with our own dogs that dry food is the most satisfactory and also is palatable to them. It does not attract flies, nor does it spoil from standing. Some dogs like their food piecemeal and enjoy returning to their dish for a few more morsels now and then. Nothing is wrong with this if you feed dry kibble.

Always be on the alert for any signs of food not agreeing with your pet, such as loss of appetite, loose stool, listlessness, loss of weight, unusual shedding, or dull coat. Of course, any of these symptoms could also be caused by other problems. Don't try to play doctor yourself or listen to a friend's advice, even though he means well. Just get yourself and your dog right over to the office of your veterinarian, then follow his advice.

Play is a very important part of your dog's life with you, no matter what his age. It is fun for him, helps him to develop his muscles and keep physically fit, and becomes a valuable means of communication between the two of you. He will learn how much fun you both can have when he retrieves a ball for you, when he carries and squeaks a toy, and when he gallops in to you from across the room or yard as you call him. When you give him his own toys, don't make the mistake of giving him an old shoe, slipper, or sock, because this only invites trouble. You'll be the one making the mistake if you punish him for ruining a new pair of shoes that you forgot to put away. He does *not* have the ability to discern the difference between the old and new property when your smell is on both!

The Outdoor Dog

So far, we've been dealing mostly with the pet that is spending much or all of his time living in the house with his family. But many dogs are happier if they spend more time, or all the time, outdoors. And some people prefer to have their pets living outdoors, at least during the day. Occasionally it is necessary to keep the dog outside if a member of the family is allergic to dogs. In such situations, make sure that the housing and living area are comfortable, weatherproof, and adequate. Your dog's house should be designed so that he is protected from storms such as driving rain and snow, and his bed should be raised off the ground to avoid dampness and cold drafts. He should have free access to an ample fenced area that should be kept clean and sanitized. Any accumulation of waste can constitute a health hazard and annoy your neighbors and friends.

Even if your dog lives outdoors, it does not mean that you will love each other less. You can schedule your time so that he will receive a certain amount of attention every day for training or for just plain loving him. He doesn't have to live inside with the family to understand how much you love him. But he will be doubly appreciative of any companionship you offer when you're home. He will always look forward to going for a walk with you or having a romp in the yard or a training session.

We mentioned the tie-out stake in the list of equipment (*see* page 22). The proper location and use of this could save your dog's life and keep you from worrying in a number of possible situations. Locate the stake where it can be left all the time, not in your way but near enough to your entrance to be convenient .

Suppose your yard is not fenced yet, or your dog is not in his fenced run. Suddenly you remember that you didn't check the burner under your beans. You have to leave him only for a minute, but in that minute he could dash away from home, perhaps into the path of a speeding car. Or maybe the telephone or front doorbell rings and you have to run to answer it. How nice for both you and your dog if you take a moment to fasten his collar to a chain attached to the stake. Make sure that you always use a flat buckled collar with your dog's identification attached. This will prevent possible accident or discomfort from a tightened, strangling collar.

As soon as you can, return and praise him, then release him. He'll soon learn that he won't be left for long, and will adjust to being restrained for short periods of time. By using the chain on the stake, your dog won't be able to free himself by chewing, and, if the collar fits properly, he won't be able to back out of it. He may protest the first few times, but he will adjust when he realizes that you will be returning soon to give him a lot of praise. *Never* forget the praise.

If you must tether your dog for slightly longer periods of time and have a shade tree, you may wish to set up a system like the one depicted in Figure 3-9. In this arrangement, there is no chance of the chain getting tangled, knotted, or shortened. Be sure to protect the trunk of the tree so that the ring cannot rub or damage it. A metal shield works well. The metal ring should be heavy enough to resist being pulled out of shape, and the shield height should be determined by your dog's height. When your dog is fastened to a chain that slides on this ring, he can go completely around, circling in either direction, without being impeded. He'll get as much exercise as he wants and will be able to follow the shade for resting and napping. The metal shield around the tree will also discourage any tendency for him to chew the tree.

SHIELD

Fig. 3-9. A metal shield will protect tree trunk from damage by ring to which a chain is fastened.

The Doghouse

Hundreds of variations of doghouse designs are available that will work for your situation, depending upon your individual preference and the size of your wallet. No matter what the design, be sure that the house conforms to the following requisites:

- constructed of weather-resistant material
- will allow cleaning and disinfecting (i.e., a lift-off roof or hinged top)
- affords ample room for moving around
- has a sleep area large enough to be comfortable and that is shielded from bad weather and protected from drafts
- has adequate ventilation
- is placed so that it faces away from the direction of prevailing winds

Diagram 3-11 depicts a regular type of doghouse mounted on top of a short post that has been set in the ground. A ring was put around the post before the house was placed in position (similar to the ring around the shade tree). This is a favorite design for dogs being trained to work in the canine units of the U.S. armed forces, and some professional kennels prefer this type.

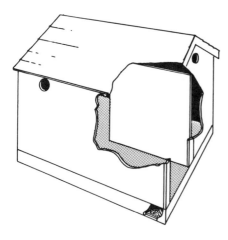

Fig. 3-10. Construction of dog house with insulating air space under flooring, and a partition to protect against drafts.

Another popular and easy design that is used chiefly by hunt-ers and farmers for their hounds and farm dogs is the barrel laid on its side and supported on a base that raises it off the damp ground. Farmers always use clean straw for bedding, and the entryway is no larger than necessary. Usually a flap of heavy material is dropped down over the opening in bad weather.

If you have a doghouse and still have not fenced the yard or a section of it for a run, you can use a wire cable and a running chain that slides along the cable from one end to the other. This can be attached to a post or tree or be stretched between two of them. You can also attach one end to a corner of the house or outbuild-ing. Mount the ends high enough so that no one will run into the cable, and stretch the cable firmly across. Be sure that the chain to which your dog's collar is attached is long enough so that your dog can enter his shelter and lie down in comfort. Make certain that you provide shade for your dog, whatever the location. Also, do not forget the "stop" on the cable. This prevents the chain from getting wrapped around the tree or post. Always plan ahead to avoid undesirable situations (see page 7, Fig. 1-2).

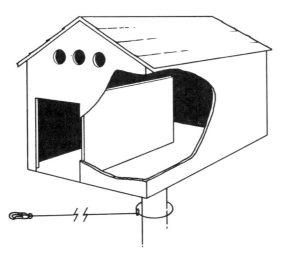

Fig. 3-11. **Dog house with anti-draft partition mounted on a short post to prevent entangled chain.**

Still another idea, and one for which we can personally vouch, makes use of the corner of a garage, barn, or outbuilding. Fencing for a run is installed to extend out from that corner. Plan the run so that it will include shade for your dog and provide an access gate for your own entry into the area.

Your dog's own kennel quarters can be built right inside the building in the corner you've selected, affording excellent protection from weather, a good bed free from drafts and raised off the floor, a clean space for his food and water, and his own doorway to go in and out as his whims may dictate. Of course, remember that you'll need a door to the kennel, too, so make it big enough for yourself!

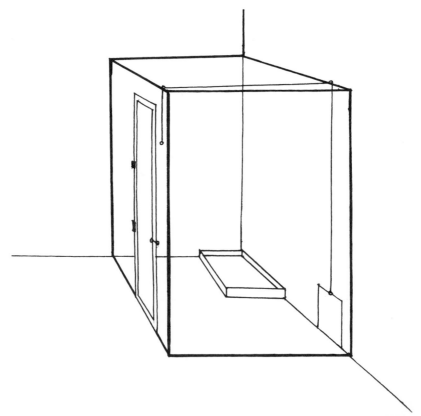

Fig. 3-12. Plan for building dog housing in a corner of garage or utility room. Note controlled slide opening into outside run. Construction may be of any suitable wire mesh or fencing.

This arrangement is unusually convenient, especially if the garage is attached to the house and the kitchen door opens into the garage. This allows easy access into the house in case you want your dog inside to keep you company part of the time. And with the garage door closed, it is a subtle way of suggesting to nosey strangers that your dog just might be in your house, and they better not trespass! Our dog actually was much happier in his own quarters than in the house with us. Of course, he had more freedom there and could go in and out as he pleased. He could also watch what was going on all around him, check on unwanted dogs and cats, eye strangers, and greet friends, all from behind the fence of his run.

Figure 3-13 illustrates one type of "doggie door" that is sold commercially. It provides an easy exit and entrance for the dog from the house to a fenced yard. When your dog is taught to use it as he pleases, everyone is happy! This particular design has a magnet at the bottom so that the door is held closed when it drops back down after your dog has gone through. It's not at all difficult to teach a dog to use it if you take it easy when you introduce him to it. Praise him each time that he makes a bit of progress toward pushing it open by himself. Perhaps it will be easier at first for you to be on one side to help and coax him and for another person to be on the other side, helping in the same way. Soon it will become a new game.

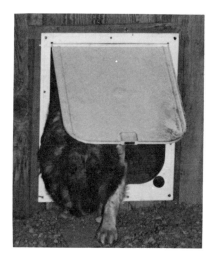

Fig. 3-13. "Doggie" door in use.

To control your dog's exits and entrances, set up a regular schedule and lock the door at certain hours. We found that housebreaking was a breeze with our Corgi when he was a puppy, just as soon as he realized that he was independent and could go and come as he pleased. Of course, he did get a bit of a shock occasionally when he found his door locked. But it never dampened his spirits or discouraged him.

————————————

Here are a few points you should consider, regardless of where your dog is housed:

- keep fresh water available in his dish
- feed on a regular time schedule
- let your dog exercise at regular times
- if on a chain, keep kinks out of it
- keep area clean, indoors or outdoors, and if you need a disinfectant, check with your vet
- in hot weather, a good hosing with cool water will help cool the whole area

If you use a little thoughtfulness and consideration in caring for your dog's comfort and health, he will be a wonderful companion for you.

Fig. 3-14. Dog on tie-out chain with swivel.

Chapter 4
BEGINNING
THE TRAINING

Dogs, just as people, need training and education, no matter how young or old, the type of breeding or genealogy, the temperament, or the size of the dog. Our aim is to give training advice that will cover nearly all existing situations of dog owners and what they desire in their dog's performance. It is your responsibility as the dog owner and trainer to select and apply the information as it pertains to your situation.

Before starting your training, you must choose a call name for your new friend. If he is eligible for registration in the American Kennel Club, you really should select two names—one to put on the form which you will send to AKC (with the proper fee) and another for your own convenience in speaking to or calling your dog. Many times the call name is a part of the registered name, but this is not necessary. As an example, we registered one dog as "Wakefield Margo's Happy Talk," and his call name is "Happy." It could just as well have been "Joe" or "Sam"—whatever suited our fancy.

When you choose the call name, keep it short, simple, and easy to say, and be sure that you will be able to put good voice inflection into it to carry your meaning (a different tone for serious work, fun, scolding). Also, be careful to avoid its sounding like any command that you may be teaching, such as: Lum—Come, Zip—Sit, Jay—Stay, Clown—Down, Rover—Over, Chump—Jump, Tuck—Hup, or Jetty—Get it!

It's extremely important for you to realize how your tone of voice influences your dog. He is very sensitive to the slightest inflection of your voice and immediately knows whether you're praising, correcting, commanding with a smile (or a frown!), hav-

ing fun, or demanding respect. Your dog will respond with pleasure, slinking, performing happily (or because he "has to"),
playing, or being obedient. It's that simple, and it means that *you*
must learn to discipline yourself and control the tone of your
voice. Practice saying some of the following simple commands,
first seriously, then with a smile, and you will be aware of the
difference in their sound: Heel, Come, Sit, Stand, Down, Stay,
Wait, Easy, Steady, Hurry Up, OK, Let's Go, Quiet, Go To Bed,
Kennel, In Your Crate, Fetch, Get (the ball, bone, etc.), Hup,
Jump, Find, Search, Give, Out, Take It, Hold, Speak, Over, Off,
Be Good, Behave, Carry, Whoa, Stop, In The Car, Track, Seek,
and your dog's name.

Praise and Correction

Understanding praise and its use will get you started on the
right track. Praise is usually thought of as physically patting your
dog, but your voice can be just as effective with the right tone. It is
important to realize that your dog may react in an entirely different way than another dog. You may get better results through
physical contact, voice tone, or perhaps a combination of the two.
Look for an enjoyable response from your dog when you praise
without his "exploding." Some dogs need only voice praise to
realize that you're pleased with their performance, while others
look for more of a show from you. We have had excellent results
by using the word "Good," but putting a lot of feeling into it by
stretching it out as "G-o-o-o-d!" You can put just as much meaning into it as you wish. If your dog needs to be patted, do it with
enough enthusiasm so that he will react happily without getting
out of control. Temper it according to what your dog likes. Always
be ready to adjust and vary the kind and amount of praise to meet
the situation. And make it a habit to praise immediately both after
a correction and when a job has been done well.

On the subject of corrections, let us present our theory and
logic as we've found it very successful. We don't believe that *any*
corrections should be administered when your dog is learning an
exercise. He should have pleasant associations with learning anything new. *After* your dog has learned through having been guided

in correct habit patterns, then deliberately makes a mistake, a well-timed correction (usually minor) is quite in order, followed immediately with praise and a return to activity and work with no time for scolding or thinking about it.

Most corrections are made with the lead and collar at the moment the mistake is made. A quick flip of the wrist and immediate release are the only actions required. Corrections on some dogs can be accomplished very effectively with just a stern tone of voice. And what we consider a severe correction administered in extreme situations, is done by controlling the lead (shortened so that it is close to the collar) with one hand, while a quick, upward slap under the jaw is given with the open fingers of the other hand, palm side up. This shocks the dog but doesn't run a risk of physical damage as a blow to the nose, muzzle, or ears might do. Again, this should be gauged according to the size and temperament of the dog. Just a little flip of a thumb or finger under the jaw of a Pomeranian can be very effective, *if* such a correction is needed. If corrections are done properly, if the timing is right, and if praise and a pleasant voice follow immediately, your dog should not be resentful and should remain a happy worker.

Lifting Your Dog

Now for another note of caution on a different subject: the recommended way to pick up a puppy or even an older dog. In both cases, size should naturally be considered. The reason for bringing this to your attention is because we're concerned about the comfort and safety of the animal, as well as about his normal development. Improper handling may physically hurt him, allow him to jump out of your grasp and break a bone or dash in front of a car, or actually put such stress on joints that it will cause a condition called "out at the elbows."

Observe Figure 4-1 and see where the hands are placed, one under the chest in front of the forelegs, the other under the hindquarters. As you lift, bring your dog toward you and cradle him against your body. He will feel secure, and you'll be confident that you're not hurting him in any way. This is about the safest, easiest, and most humane way to lift a dog. Never relax your hold, but don't tighten it to the point that your pup hurts from being squeezed. Strike a happy medium. Don't try to imitate the scruff-of-the-neck carry that a mother dog sometimes uses to move her newborn puppies. They're not heavy at that age, and besides, she is instinctively aware of how to do it and how much pressure is needed.

Your Dog and Strangers

When your dog must meet other members of the family, it's very important (from your dog's point of view) that his interests are taken into consideration when he's introduced to them. The first basic rule for everyone to remember is: don't ever force yourself on a dog in trying to make friends with him. Let *him* make the advances, not you.

If you notice that your dog is reluctant or actually afraid of a person, try to figure out why. Perhaps that person has an odor that arouses suspicion or is distasteful to the dog. It could be perfume, nicotine from cigarettes, alcohol, or a fear scent, or perhaps a harsh voice or rough, rowdy handling that frightens the dog. Eliminate or take corrective action on the problem as soon as possible so that your dog will relax with the family and have a happy environment. Let him take his own time to make up with

Fig. 4-1. Correct way to hold a puppy.

each family member. Assure him with your own actions toward the others that you're all one big happy family that lives together in harmony and that there is no need for distrust, especially toward you.

One way of building up your dog's trust in the others is to ask them to take turns giving him food and water, playing games with him, and taking him out to exercise. It's not advisable for a dog to be entirely dependent on just one individual. In case you have to be away for an emergency, your dog can suffer if he feels that he must have his food and water only from you. It could result in tragedy for both of you.

Training Equipment

Before we take the plunge and get into training, let us check the equipment that you'll need. Supplies are usually available at pet stores, pet departments in stores, or through obedience training classes.

First on the list is the collar and lead. We prefer, especially for puppies, a plain buckled collar of flat leather or woven fabric (such as nylon). If your new charge has not been lead-broken, you'll need a short length of rope (like a clothesline) about one and one-half times the length of his body. The lead should be of a light pliable leather or a narrow-width (no more than one-half inch), strong woven fabric, such as a webbing, from four to six feet long. A tie-out stake will complete your immediate needs. This is made like a corkscrew for ease of putting it into the ground and comes with a length of metal chain and snap for attaching to the collar. This is used only as a temporary tether for your dog, usually when he's not under your supervision, and the metal chain is necessary to prevent him from chewing to set himself free.

Be sure that the collar can be adjusted for a snug fit, but do not make it tight. However, don't adjust it loose enough so that he can back out of it! Remember that you need to be in control at all times, but this doesn't mean that your pal need be uncomfortable. All collars have a ring for attaching the snap of the lead. The "slip training collar" (some refer to it as a choke collar) has two rings, the collar being formed by pulling it through one of them. When the lead is attached to one of the rings and is pulled up, the collar gets smaller and will tighten around a dog's neck. We refer to this as the "working" or "live" ring. When it's attached to the other ring, it does not tighten but acts like a plain collar. We call this the "non-working" or "dead" ring and recommend it over the "live" ring except in specific unusual circumstances, when a definite correction is required (see Figs. 4-3 and 4-4).

Fig. 4-2. Nylon slip collar.

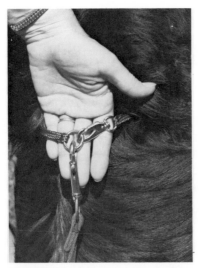

Fig. 4-3. Collar in non-working position.

Fig. 4-4. Collar in "choke" or "live" position.

Beginning Lessons

Sit and Stand—Your first step will be teaching your dog the commands Stand and Sit, associating each word every time with the repetition of the performance. We'll do this in one place with no forward motion involved. Your dog will not only start to learn the meaning of these two words, he will also begin to understand what you want when he feels you exert a slight pressure on the collar.

First choose a comfortable spot for yourself, sitting, squatting, or kneeling on the floor, or sitting in a chair or on a hassock. If it's difficult for you to bend down and you have a small dog, you can put your dog on a higher level, such as on a bench or table. If you plan to teach your dog to heel, or walk at your left side (and this is a must if you ever plan to compete in any dog obedience competition that follows the rules set up by the American Kennel Club), place your dog in front of you with his head facing to your right, tail toward your left. If you have a definite reason for wanting your dog to work at your right side, then reverse his position in front of you.

Take hold of your dog's collar with the hand nearest his head, placing your fingers around it so that the back of your hand is

Fig. 4-5. Use pressure on collar and above the hocks to encourage puppy to sit.   **Fig. 4-6. The Sit accomplished.**

against his body. Practice sliding your hand from underneath his chin to up behind his head and back again, keeping your hand around the collar in the original position. Tell your dog Steady as you move your hand around in the collar. With your dog standing, and using your other hand as the guide, slide your hand gently over his back and down over the hindquarters to the hocks. At this point, apply a little pressure *up* and *back* with the collar (from behind the head), and, at the same time, press in above both hocks with the other hand and say Sit. It is almost like squeezing an accordion, and your dog will practically sit right down on your hand. This is done with very little effort on your part, even with large dogs, and teaches your dog what you want of him by showing him rather than by using unpleasant force. Be careful not to "judo chop" across the hocks!

To take him out of the Sit and get him to Stand, slide your collar hand to under his chin, and put your other hand under his belly with the *back* of your hand toward his body and just ahead of his hind leg. Working both hands together, pull forward with the collar and lift with the other hand, giving the command Stand. Wasn't that easy? In doing both the Sit and the Stand, equalize the pressure that you apply with both hands as you go into action. As

Fig. 4-7. The puppy learns to stand.

your dog begins to learn what you are teaching him, gradually start to eliminate the help you're giving with the hand at the hocks and under the belly, teaching him to respond to the command along with a slight pressure on the collar. Practice this three to five times at one session, then do another activity to take his mind off of it.

You'll notice that all the commands are simple, single words. Be sure to praise your dog each time that he and you accomplish an exercise or part of an exercise. Never continue training to the point of tiring or boring your friend, and keep the tone of your voice happy. Smile! Just a word of caution: do not try to go too fast from one position to the other, because you want to encourage steadiness on both commands. Just take it easy. Also (and we know this from personal experience), beware of losing your temper and becoming frustrated during *any* training session. You'll accomplish nothing, your dog will suffer from it, and you'll lose ground in whatever you had accomplished previously. If you find this happening, cut your training immediately for that day and literally apologize to your dog. He'll understand and will be anxious to work the next time, *after* you have composed yourself.

Walking on Lead—If your dog has not been taught to walk on lead, you will start him by attaching the short length of rope to his collar. This will avoid his resenting being pulled one way and another by you and blaming you for it. He will learn that he's doing it to himself. It's best to do this outside, where you can oversee his actions without participating yourself. Fasten the rope to his collar and let him go on his own. Pay no attention to him if he comes to you or expects you to help him out of his problem, and discourage his depending upon you for help. Let him work it out by himself.

He'll probably be annoyed and perhaps confused with the rope getting in his way, especially if he steps on it and trips himself! He probably won't like the feeling that he gets when it tightens and pulls on the collar. He may even growl at it or try to bite it to rid himself of the pesky thing. He may get tired and lie down, giving some thought to what his next line of attack should be. Don't worry about him, he'll be OK. Soon he will get the idea that he can avoid stepping on the rope and not feel the pull on his collar. At this point, you can pick up the end of the rope and walk with him. Notice that we say walk *with him,* not make him walk with you.

Now he'll be associating your nearness, your footstep vibrations, and your conversational voice with his own moving, still having this "attachment" on his collar. When he gets used to this situation, introduce a little tension on the rope, using only your fingers to apply it. Call his name and praise him as he responds to it, and use the word "G-o-o-o-o-d!" He'll love it! If you think that he needs more time with the rope dragging, drop it again and let him go. Don't change to the regular lead until he will let you apply tension to the rope without resenting it.

The length of the lead can be from four to six feet. If you're tall and your dog is short, probably the six-foot length will be more appropriate and easier to handle. By the same token, if your dog is fairly tall and you're not, a lot of lead in your hand is superfluous and just in your way. We like to use both hands on the lead in training, one hand to hold the lead out of the way and the other (on the dog's side) to guide him and show him what you want him to do.

Whenever you have a training session on lead, aim for the dog's attention and use his name as you introduce turns to the right and left, about turns, and change of pace (slow, normal, fast), and vary your patterns to keep the lesson interesting. Keep it fun for both of you and do not let him get tired or bored.

He should soon start to realize that he must pay attention and heed a slight pressure on the collar, along with your tone of voice, and begin to understand the meaning of certain words. Most people, by the way, use the word, Heel, as their command for their dog to stay in position at their side while moving. Your dog will give you good attention if you keep your training peppy, if you talk and praise him as you're moving, and if you keep him guessing as to what comes next, not allowing him to fall into a pattern routine. If you need to bring his attention back to you, give a slight, quick correction with the least amount of movement possible on your part, just a flip of your wrist. Be sure that your lead is shortened or folded up well as you work so that you don't have to go into any extra motions that serve only as unnecessary distractions. A dog is always attracted by movement, so do away with motions you don't need.

Keep your training session short and interesting. Don't be afraid to break the work periods by having fun, teaching tricks, going for a short ride, or just resting. It can do you both good, and you can resume with a much better outlook and accomplish more in the end.

Tying Your Dog—The tie-out stake should be used only as an emergency piece of equipment for fastening your dog outside if you have to leave him for a few minutes to answer the telephone, take the cake out of the oven, turn the coffeepot on, or whatever. But you do need to use a little common sense to introduce him to it before you just snap his collar onto it and leave him. It can be a very frustrating experience for him if not done right.

He'll need to be assured that it is all right for him to be left alone in the yard and that you'll return shortly. His being by himself is the reason for using the metal chain, because he might decide to chew a lead or rope in half and be off, perhaps into dangerous traffic or other pitfalls.

Choose a location where you will be able to observe his activity from inside, and screw the stake into the ground. Make sure that it is in a clear area so that he will not immediately wind himself around a tree, bush, or post. Choose a command to teach him, such as Be Good or Wait For Me, and be consistent, always using this command when you snap the chain on his collar.

The first time that you put him on the tie-out, do it during one of your training sessions, when you've really been enjoying yourselves. Don't make a big deal out of it. Just treat it as an ordinary activity as you take him over, remove your lead, and fasten the chain. *Never* fasten the chain on the live ring if you are using a slip collar. A regular buckled collar is really the only safe collar for tying your dog, so it is better to change the collar unless you are already working with the buckled collar.

Give him the command and some praise and go inside, even though he may be fussing and crying. Just ignore his protests, and return to his rescue only if he needs to be untangled from the chain. Watch him from your vantage point, and you'll see him calm down when he realizes that nobody is watching his antics. He probably will even get tired and resigned to the situation and proceed to take a nap.

This is your cue to go outside and enthusiastically show your happiness over his performance. Clap your hands and go to him, giving him lots of praise. Take him off the chain, put him back on your lead, and resume your practice session. Don't give him a romp immediately after his being on the tie-out stake. Let him associate it with work sessions rather than play and games. Remember: this should be relied upon as a lifesaving piece of equipment, so use it well.

Fig. 4-8. A well-trained dog is under control when taken for walks.

Chapter 5
HOME TRAINING

Housebreaking

About the most important lesson to teach your dog at the beginning is to become clean in his habits while living in your home with you. Sometimes this can be a serious project, particularly if you have an older dog that has not yet learned what is right and wrong. But if you approach the training with logic, and if you try to understand your dog, it need not be an insurmountable task.

It was instinctual for wild dogs of long ago to mark their territory with their urine scent to let other animals know that they were ready to protect it. Sometimes we still find our dogs following this instinct, but it is usually quite easy to teach them that the house is not the place to display such behavior. Even though many effective cleaners are available, we don't like to use them if we can avoid it, and the way to avoid it is to prevent it from happening. We are bound to face it once in awhile, because mistakes do happen, especially in case of illness.

A collapsible wire crate is the most ideal aid for fast and effective housebreaking. It should become your dog's bed, rest area, and security corner. Although other crate designs are available, we like this one because it allows the dog to see what is going on around him. He doesn't feel as though he has been put out of sight and is being punished. It gives him confidence. Never use the crate right after a harsh scolding or severe correction. It is his home and should be regarded as a desirable place. Do not let him associate it with anything that he resents.

The size of the crate should be determined by the mature size of your dog. He should be able to stand up inside it and lie down in comfort, but it should not be large enough to allow him to roam around in it. If you wait for your puppy to grow a bit larger before purchasing a crate, you can compensate by using a small room (the kitchen is usually good because it's easy to clean and you can be around to keep an eye on him). Put expansion gates at the doorways to confine him to that one room. Cover the floor with newspapers, right to the outside door. When using the crate and the gates, leave the crate door open so that your dog is free to go in and out as he wishes. Seldom will a dog soil his own bed before going out and using the papers. As the papers become soiled, pick them up and remove them, and clean and disinfect the area involved. Do not replace these papers, except those that are near the outside door exit. This will encourage your dog to look for a paper to use and gradually will get him into the habit of going to the door when he has to relieve himself. Close the door to his crate only when necessary for his own protection or when he goes to sleep.

When the only remaining paper is by the door, your dog has almost learned his lesson. Now it is up to you to time his trips to the door, then *out* the door, *before* he has a chance to do any soiling. Regulate him by the schedule of his meals, drinking behavior, and naps. When taking him out to do his duty, always take him to where he eliminated previously. Let him know how good he was by your own exuberance. Later, you can teach him to speak, then combine it with going out the door, thus getting him to speak to be taken outside.

If your dog is fully grown and not housebroken, follow the same procedure of teaching him that the crate is his bed, his own corner to which he can go at any time. You can confine him when you are unable to keep an eye on him until he is completely housebroken. It's especially advisable to put him in his crate for a short while after he eats, because it usually takes a little time for the digestive process to work and give him the signal that it is time to go outside. It is unusual for a grown dog to soil his own bed, but don't expect too much from him. Don't see how long he can hold it. Cooperate with him, read his desires by his behavior, and he'll cooperate with you.

Many people, including ourselves, train our dogs to go on command. If you use the same word or phrase each time that you take him out to "exercise" (eliminate), he will soon catch on to the idea of the purpose of the trip outside. We always use the phrase

"Hurry Up!" but there are countless words and phrases that can be chosen.

As your dog becomes more reliable and starts to indicate that he wants to go outside by speaking, whining, or going to the door, you can begin to relax your constant vigil and let him free, at first for short periods, in other rooms of the house where he is allowed. Then you can extend the time to longer stretches, depending upon your dog's reactions. Remember: once you have failed to let him out in time and caused him to have an accident, he will likely return again to the same spot and repeat his mistake, no matter how thoroughly you clean it. The blame will be on *you*, not on your dog.

Familiarity with Household Activities

As long as your dog is going to be your house companion, he should become familiar with appliances and other equipment so that he will not be frightened by any of them. You should introduce him to them gradually and in a sensible manner. Never show fear or bad emotion in your dog's presence, because his senses are very keen. He'll realize how you feel and will be affected by it. Television programs and the radio seldom have a disturbing effect on your dog except when he hears a dog barking, a wolf howling, or occasionally other animal sounds. Don't yell at your dog for this. Tell him that everything is OK and reassure him, but do not dwell upon it.

When you get out the vacuum cleaner for the first time, watch your dog closely. Turn on the cleaner and let it run. Talk to your dog, then leave and let him investigate it by himself. If he's at all curious, he will do just that. Come back and praise him, using a reassuring tone of voice. Never tease him with it, like pushing the nozzle toward him, for you may create more of a problem than you can handle.

Your dog can become accustomed to your kitchen appliances just by watching you as you operate them. Don't chase him away. Let him know that they won't cause any harm. Once he gets used to the different noises and sees you not being bothered by any of them, he won't even show any interest in them.

In the case of a flash camera, it is very important that your dog see it operate *before* you try to take a picture of him. In other words, let him see it from the side or in back and get used to that before you come toward him from in front. Always use that reassuring tone of voice and give plenty of praise whenever your dog is experiencing something new.

Another object that a dog, especially a puppy, should be shown is a mirror. This is interesting to watch because he's usually baffled. He seems to think that another puppy must be there somewhere, but he can't find it. And there is no smell or noise to help him locate that pup. If you do this with an older dog, take no chances of exciting him and having him bolt, becoming aggressive and attacking the mirror, or going overboard in any way. Put him on lead and approach the mirror slowly, talking to him as you go. Kneel down by him and praise him, get him to relax, and be patient. If, on a second approach, you still get the same reaction to the "strange" dog in the mirror, reach out and touch the mirror dog and laugh, start to loosen the lead, and let him come up to it as you're touching it. He is still under control on the lead. Praise him now with the same hand that you used to touch the mirror. Laugh and make a big deal out of it, then walk away. Release the lead, turn toward the mirror, and see how he reacts. If he is now comfortable, you'll know that your lesson has been successful. Repeat the procedure another day if necessary. Soon you will see that it is "old hat" to him and just another piece of furniture!

Controlling Your Dog

"Controlled walking" means just what it says. You are not demanding a certain position in relation to you, just that your dog behave well on lead and go with you where *you* want to go without a lot of pulling and hauling. You will use this in teaching your dog to go through doors and gates and to go on balconies and up and down stairs.

When your dog goes through a door or gate for the first time, make sure that it opens *away* from you, whether it is glass, solid, or screen. This will avoid any panic from fear of being hit by an object that he does not understand. Keep his lead short so that he stays close to you. Laugh and give him an OK command as you guide him through while holding the door open. Be sure that you hold the door open until he's safely through, and don't let it slam shut behind him. Sudden, sharp noises behind a dog can be traumatic, and it requires much time and patience to overcome them. Be especially careful when you return, with the door opening toward you. Keep your dog in a position so that *you* will have to move out of the way when the door is opened. Guide your dog through when the way is clear and safe. He will soon learn when it is all right to move and when it is not. And to avoid having your dog get excited and run into a glass or screen door, put decals on them at your *dog's eye* level.

If your dog will be spending any time on a balcony, even with adequate railing, introduce him to it on lead to teach him that he is *not* to try to jump over or go between the posts of the railing. Keep your lead short and slightly snug to prevent his carrying out any crazy ideas he might have about chasing another dog or a squirrel. Let him look and sniff and investigate all he wants. He'll gain confidence this way and realize that you're there to help him if he needs you.

Fig. 5-1. Hold door away from dog as you go through.

Fig. 5-2. Introduce the dog carefully to balcony.

Now some advice on teaching your dog to go up and down stairs. Granted, some dogs don't have to be taught because they figure it out for themselves without any help. But others are scared stiff and are completely baffled when faced with stairs for the first time. If done right, your pup will gain all the confidence he needs in a very short time.

Let's assume that you are going to teach a puppy or a small dog. First you must teach him to go *down* the steps, because he can see what lies ahead of him from this position. If you have to start from the bottom, first *carry* him up three or four steps and work from there. Do not expect him to face a long flight of stairs at the beginning. Use only the collar, holding it with one hand and guiding and steadying your dog with the other. Stay in front of him and start backing down, one step at a time. Encourage him and take it slowly, but control him so that he does not try to jump. If necessary, show him that it's OK to move his feet a little at a time. Once he starts on his own, keep him going, but don't drag or force him. All you need to do is *show* him and praise him by talking and encouraging with a pleasant tone of voice. Two or three times down the steps in this manner and your pup will be ready to show you how much he's learned.

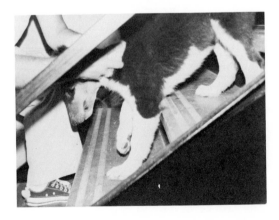

Fig. 5-3. Hold his collar and steady dog as you teach him to manipulate stairs.

Going up the steps is a bit different, because your dog cannot see what is beyond, above his eye level. It's unknown, and he has to gain confidence in himself to find out "what's up there." He depends upon you, knowing that you won't make him do anything that will bring him harm. In this case, you will have to go up the steps backwards, or slide up each step. If it will be easier, put a lead on your dog but hold it as close to the collar as possible. Use a little pressure on the collar as needed and help him up the first step. Coax him and talk with him the rest of the way. Get up three

Fig. 5-4. Your dog should learn to walk in heel position without forging as you go up or down stairways.

or four steps, turn around, and carefully guide him back down, keeping the lead short. When down, walk back up this time, staying only about one-half step ahead of your pup. Don't let him try to jump. Keep him calm and steady. Now try going both up and down with your dog on a loose lead, controlling him with your voice alone. Then take a rest, you earned it. From now on, every time that you and your pup are on stairs, his confidence will increase and you will not have to worry about his safety, *if* you've done a good teaching job.

If you are training an older and larger dog, it will be much easier because he can see where he's going. You will need to control the collar in the same manner and take it easy, one step at a time. The larger dogs usually learn faster, but be careful that their confidence doesn't build *too fast.* Don't let them get the idea that they can bolt in either direction or pull you up or down stairs when on lead. If you encounter this problem, stop the dog's motion, go to a very short lead, and start again. Don't let him boss you! Three to five times of this exercise at one training is sufficient. Do not overdo it—enough is enough. You both want to stay happy and be good friends.

One important decision that you should make at the beginning is how much freedom of the house you will allow your dog. Will he be barred from the dining room, from the living room, from the furniture? Is he to be allowed in the dining room except when you are having a meal? Is he to be allowed on certain pieces of furniture and not on others? This will all enter into his training, and *all* members of the family need to make these decisions and be consistent in carrying them out. Remember to introduce your pup to the other rooms gradually and always under supervision. You can return him to his crate if necessary, but not for punishment if he's made a mistake. If you watch him as you should, you can prevent such incidents, and he will learn what he may do with your approval.

Later on, you will be playing games with him and teaching him tricks. His restrictions about the house will more or less dictate the extent of these activities. To make it easier for yourself, let him explore his new territory one room at a time, provided you have doors that can be closed or barricaded. This way, you won't have to follow him to keep an eye on him.

Toys

Any dog, regardless of age or size, needs toys that he knows are his own. Dogs love to have their own things just as children do. They can entertain themselves by the hour, especially if they are encouraged and think that they're amusing you as well as themselves. Give each toy a name and always refer to it by that name. Also, provide a box or receptacle for the toys and let your puppy know that he is free to go to it and choose his own toy. Soon he'll begin to associate the name with the particular toy and you can ask him to get his ball (doll, bone, mouse, dumbbell, or other toy). Go overboard with praise when he starts bringing the right ones to you. Don't encourage any tug-of-war games. Your dog may develop poor habits, such as grabbing objects out of your hand or snapping. Teach him to "give" his toy to you when he brings it for a play session.

One note of advice regarding squeak toys: if you leave one with him in his crate at night, you'll have only yourself to blame when you are awakened by the noise long before you're ready to get dressed and take him outside. And if you let him get away with it once, he will try it every time he has the chance.

Fig. 5-5. All dogs enjoy toys.

Understanding Your Dog's Senses

We probably will never fully understand the inner workings of a dog's mind and exactly why he responds the way he does, because every dog is unique. The combination of genes, different in each individual, means that we must study each one with an open mind and learn to observe those differences.

Dogs are blessed with the same set of senses as humans—sight, hearing, touch, taste, and smell—and they also have the brain that puts all the senses to work. Of course, the big difference is that some of their senses are so highly developed that it's impossible to compare them with human traits. Their sense of smell is beyond our comprehension. Some dogs' scenting ability has been estimated by researchers as being one million times greater than that of a person, and these results have been measured by scientific instruments.

Many times, a dog's reactions cannot even be traced to any of the five senses, and we fully believe that the only explanation is a sixth sense, or ESP (extrasensory perception). Much study has been put into this phase of dog behavior since many such reactions have been reported for which there have been no satisfactory explanations. As you and your dog grow closer in your relationship and understanding of one another, you will very likely come to the same conclusion—that certain things are just not explainable in any other way.

Sense of Smell—The following list gives you an idea of the many ways in which the dog's sense of smell helps him to function.

- distrust of one whose body gives off a fear scent
- ease of finding his own food, water, and toys
- alerting the presence of another dog or animal
- ability to separate one type of animal scent from another
- ability to separate one person's scent from another
- ability to detect, select, and identify certain types of scent through training, such as the scent of gunpowder, metallic materials, or drugs.

Sense of Hearing—We all realize that a dog's hearing is much more acute than that of a person. It seems that *our* dog will become alert when a leaf falls or turns over! Other hearing capabilities of dogs include:

- recognizing the approach of your car by its motor sound
- recognizing different whistles and their meaning
- knowing the meaning behind different tones of voice—happiness, confidence, fear, punishment
- recognizing footsteps of people who they know
- being suspicious or afraid of sounds such as thunder, gunshots, the slamming of a door, a high-pitched siren.

Sense of Seeing—Next we'll consider a dog's eyes and some of their limitations. Much research has been conducted in this field, and most scientists have concluded that a dog's world is composed of shades of gray, from black to white. They claim that dogs respond to color intensity in their tests and not to actual differences in the color. We know from our personal experiences with many puppies that it is usually the bright red or fluorescent orange ball that attracts them in play. Occasionally, a puppy has preferred to play with a medium blue ball.

Regardless of how dogs see color, we do know that what attracts their attention first is *motion,* even at great distances. You can run a test on this yourself. Choose a spot a good distance away but where you can be seen by your dog, making sure that your scent is not being carried toward him by the wind. Be sure that he doesn't watch you go, and stand still. He will be able to see you, but he won't recognize you *until* you start to move. Then he'll let you know that you are not fooling *him.*

A dog can also judge distance very well, as proven in training for performance in obedience competition at dog shows. A dog can jump both the high and long jumps. He knows just how much thrust he needs to clear both types. In field trials, a dog is trained to watch and "mark" the location of a fallen bird, and once sent to retrieve, he gets direction signals at a distance from his handler. It is a revelation to observe the performances of the dogs entered in field trials. Dogs that are trained for herding are also amazing for what they can discern at great distances, especially when any motion is involved. Their eyes are one of their most important assets in herding.

Your dog can also visually interpret your own facial expressions of scowling, glaring, or smiling and know whether you are displeased, upset, or happy. You may find the peripheral vision of some dogs limited due to the physical location of their eyes in the head. They are quick to observe motion as long as the object is in the scope of their vision. When the object goes out of sight, they turn their attention elsewhere.

Dependence on vision and quickness to react to what he sees, according to his degree of training and his natural talent, is what determines whether a guide dog is dependable for a blind person. A guide dog must learn to see and react to many situations, such as obstacles, curb steps, stairs, doorways, gates, bad footing, an overhanging object that may interfere with a person's progress, moving carts, and moving traffic. If you have an opportunity to watch a team of dog and handler at close range, you can actually *see* them think.

Senses of Touch and Taste—These two senses do not play such important roles in the behavior of a dog, and we understand them more easily. We take advantage of touch every time that we pet our dogs, groom them, or praise them through bodily contact. And it's easy to see how important taste is to them when they're fed. It is *not* a good idea to indulge them with human food. Many commercial dog foods are perfectly balanced for them as a complete diet and are also palatable. If your dog has a particular physical problem, let your veterinarian advise you as to the best diet for your dog.

Instincts—Dogs are born with instincts, many of which can be traced back to before man domesticated the dog. It is sometimes difficult to differentiate between reactions and determine whether they are caused by training and environment or instinct and inheritance. Some instinctual actions include:

- self-protection from people and other animals
- protection of home, property, owner, and family

- alerting to danger, unusual sounds, smoke
- devotion to family and animal friends
- acceptance of life conditions in general
- self-preservation, ability to find life-sustaining elements if necessary
- to treat minor wounds
- making a bed by circling until it is "just right" before lying down, as though he were softening the material by working it with his feet.

Signs of Behavioral Problems

Some of the signals that will tell you something is wrong are:

- unusual or abnormal ear carriage
- change of eye color indicates illness, aggression
- blowing of flews (lips) warns of danger, fight
- inability to relax shows confusion, uncertainty
- shyness shows incomplete introduction to whatever brings this reaction
- resentment of any number of things and/or people—analysis of "why" is called for here (voice, type of correction, sounds, smell of tobacco, perfume, alcohol)
- confusion, sometimes caused by being left alone, ignored, yelled at, corrected long after a mistake so that no association is made
- fear shown by hiding, crying, urinating when touched, running away
- fear of newspapers, magazines, fly swatter, after having been punished with them.

If you think about these problems and use a bit of logic, you will realize that your dog is not a machine or robot. You can't drop a quarter in a slot and solve your problems and those of your dog. There is no such thing as "instant training." It takes time, study, patience, and understanding, as well as humane training to develop your dog into the kind of companion that you'd like to have.

Points To Remember

Before we get you started into serious, but basic, training, read and study the following points of advice. Most of them apply at all times, no matter if you're just beginning or think that you have completed your dog's training. *Don't let him:*

- walk on a harness if he enjoys pulling
- leap in or out of cars, trucks, boats
- jump at windows (car or house)
- bolt up or down stairs
- play with training equipment, clothing
- chew on his lead
- interfere with your own walking
- on *all* furniture; save some for company
- jump fences or hedges
- beg for and accept food from the table
- become afraid of you
- chase cars, cycles or other vehicles
- learn to fear strangers to whom you are talking
- be handled by everyone, just those whom you know and trust
- be teased and manhandled by people
- take food from everybody.

And do not brag about how your dog fears you, or make unnecessary corrections. Remember—do not listen to everyone who claims to be an EXPERT. As long as dogs and people continue to be born, there will be individuals with unique personalities. No one can be an expert on every individual. Our favorite definition of an "expert:" An "ex" is a has-been, and a "spurt" is a drip under pressure!

Chapter 6
BASIC TRAINING
ON LEAD

Before beginning, you and your family should reach agreement on several points so that your dog will not become confused. Your family must cooperate; otherwise, the training will suffer and your dog will lose confidence in everyone.

The training will also be influenced by the reason you got your dog in the first place. But in all cases, training is necessary if you're going to enjoy him and he's going to enjoy working for you. For instance, if you plan to compete in obedience classes at dog shows, your dog *must* heel at your left side. In bird hunting, most dogs heel on the opposite side from where the gun shells are ejected, which is usually determined by the handler being left- or right-handed. If working for the police or handicapped, no sit in front would be taught because the possibility of an accident is obvious. For anyone in a wheelchair or using canes, crutches, or a walker, the dog can be taught to heel on either side, depending upon which is easier and more satisfactory. If the handler is blind or has poor vision in one eye, teach the dog to heel on the side with the good eye. If a blind handler uses a white cane, it would be more sensible and safer to teach the dog to heel on the side away from the cane. When using a dog in hunting and retrieving, it is optional as to whether he is taught to sit in front or go directly to heel position before releasing the retrieved game. A retriever should never be allowed to play a game of tug-of-war because it tends to develop a "hard" mouth, which is not good for bird work. And if the handler is elderly, the dog should learn to adjust his pace automatically, with no unnecessary guiding or correcting.

---

*Editor's Note: If you have a handicap, we suggest you read Chapter 7, 8, or 9, as appropriate, before reading Chapter 6.

The Ground Rules

The following points should be remembered when you begin to train your dog:

- Try to avoid using the word No as a command. A substitute with the same meaning could be "nein."
- Everyone working or playing with the dog must use the same commands for the same activities. Put yourself in your dog's place and think how confused you would be if you were told "Come" by one, "Come over here" by another, "Get over here" by a third and were called just by your name by a fourth.
- Feeding and exercise time should be on an organized, regular schedule.
- Give your dog praise by both bodily contact (petting) and by a pleasant tone of voice.
- Any corrections should be given only with the lead and collar and the tone of voice. If a more severe correction is needed, the open fingers of your hand may be used for an *upward* slap *under* his chin.
- Remember to smile when training; never glare at your dog or stamp your feet. This is not the time to display your temper.
- To prepare him for any sudden or sharp noises, first let him hear them from in front and not close to him. The same applies to flash cameras. Be sure to give your dog plenty of praise.
- It's good to play games with your dog, but remember to let *him* win.
- Teach him tricks if you wish, *show* him what you want using your hands and motion, and encourage with a good tone of voice.
- Don't expect too much from him in a short time, especially if he is a puppy.
- When you're having fun, be sure that you show it yourself with laughter, enthusiasm, praise, and lots of motion.

Heel

Now that everyone has agreed to follow the ground rules, let's get started on our actual training, first concentrating on teaching what the command Heel means, on lead and in motion. Attach the snap at the end of your lead to the dead or non-working ring of the training collar or the regular ring on a buckled collar.

Heel position means that your dog works at your side and in no way interferes with your movements, no matter in what direction you move or at what pace. In teaching this position, try not to allow your dog's shoulder to be ahead of your leg on the side where he is heeling. If you have the use of both hands, this will be easy, no matter which side your dog works on.

For practicing, hold your lead with both hands, one close to your dog's collar and the other keeping the remaining lead gathered out of the way so that you have good control. The controlling hand (nearest your dog) should never be raised above your waist, because you lose a great deal in timing when your lead is longer than necessary. All you need for good control is a snap of your wrist, either back, forward, or up and back, depending on the situation.

Fig. 6-1. The Heel position on the handler's left side.

Fig. 6-2. Heel position on the handler's right side.

Having taught the sit and stand commands in beginning train-ing, you can now put them to good use. Use the hand nearest to your dog to let him know where you want him, and give the commands as needed. When you move ahead, go just a short way each time, keeping his attention and making an effort to keep the training pleasurable. Let him know that it will be fun to work with you.

We cannot overstress the importance of *using your dog's name* to get his attention before giving him a moving command. For instance, when starting to heel, first give his name, then the command Heel as you start your motion, leading out first with the foot nearest your dog (his "guide foot"). Be careful to control your lead and encourage your dog with a pleasant tone of voice. Move forward a few feet and come to a halt, using his name and the command Sit. If you are walking normally, without aid, it will help your dog to sit in the right position as you halt if you stop on the foot *away* from him, making the foot *nearest* him the *last* one in motion. This is the foot that he uses as his guide. Try to get your timing down so that your command, Sit, is just before that last motion stops.

Be sure to praise your dog as soon as he sits. Bodily contact praise is usually the best in this situation because it will help to bring your dog near you. When you're moving, maintain a steady flow of pleasant conversation.

If your dog forges ahead of you while walking on lead, bring your lead around behind your body and hold it steady in that position, or fasten it to your waist. It's much easier for your body to absorb the shock of a sudden lunge rather than your hands and arms, especially if you are handicapped and using a walker or cane. It is also a very effective method for a small person to use to control a large or rambunctious dog. With this method, you won't need to worry about your dog being in command and having *you* on the end of the lead.

If you are on one or two crutches while training, you must make your own decision as to where you want your dog to work. If you're not planning to show your dog in obedience competition, then choose your stronger side or the one more comfortable for you.

If you have impaired eyesight, choose the side on which you have the best peripheral vision. Remember that a dog is affected by motion; therefore body movement, caused by your turning your head towards him, should be eliminated as much as possible. This can cause your dog to lag and go away from your side.

If you have a voice problem, you may have to learn how to give and teach visual signals, such as Heel, Stand, Down, Come, Sit, and Go to Heel or Finish if your dog comes and sits in front of you. A number of books on training formal obedience, including instruction on the use of hand signals, are available (See bibliography).

When you start practicing turns, take it easy and don't try any spectacular, sharp pivoting. You can try that later if you wish, but you must think of your dog's viewpoint *first*. Make your turn right or left like a small arc until your dog gets the idea and starts to respond well. Say just his name for attention as you start the turn. Practice your first turns *away* from your dog, and gradually make your turning arc smaller until you can go into a pivot-type turn. Remember to talk to your dog and praise him with "G-o-o-o-o-d!"

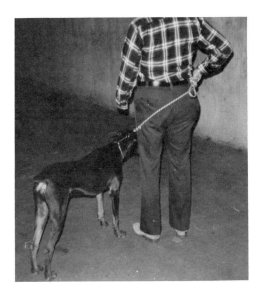

Fig. 6-3. To prevent dog from forging bring lead around behind your back.

When you start making turns toward your dog, call his name and be ready to restrain him a bit with the lead. Don't jerk or snap it, however. Start your arc slowly, and vary your heeling patterns as you progress, alternating with straight stretches of heeling and changing the direction of the turns. The more variety in your training, the easier it will be for you to keep your dog's attention.

In doing the about turn, do it *away* from your dog. This prevents any chance of your bumping into him with your feet or aids before he fully understands how far away he has to remain to keep out of the way. Experience, practice, and understanding are necessary for your dog to learn the right pattern for his heeling on this about turn, which simply means that you're turning halfway around and heading back the same way from which you came. Don't try to turn fast. Work with your dog, talk to him, guide him, and remember that magic word—"G-o-o-o-o-d!" as the turn is completed. Then continue on in a straight line.

A word of caution: no training session should ever become an endurance contest! This applies to both you and your dog. When tired or bored, interest fades and resentment begins. A good rule to follow in all your training is to never repeat any part of a lesson more than three to five times before going on to another activity.

Fig. 6-5. The dog should remain in position as you reverse direction in an about turn.

As we all know, you will not always be moving at the same pace when heeling your dog, so it's necessary to teach him to remain in the desired position at your side, regardless of pace. Your lead control, your dog's attention, and a pleasant attitude on your part are all important. Changing pace occurs in your every-day livng, when you go out to enjoy the fresh air, work in the field (hunt), or enter competition at a dog show.

When changing from a normal pace to a slow or fast pace, do it gradually. Don't break abruptly from one speed to another. Try to keep rhythm in your moving; don't let it become jerky.

If you have been using a guide on your wheelchair or walker, find out how well your dog has learned his heeling lessons before you continue your training. Remove just the L-shaped portion that extends back and to the outside of his body, but keep it available for later use. Now try the heeling and the turns with the lead fastened or with you holding it, whichever is easier. You can always put this section of the aid back on if you feel your dog isn't ready to work without its help. (See next chapter for more complete details.)

Stay and Wait

The Stay and Wait commands are very important, and their use is unlimited. They are not interchangeable, as each one has its separate meaning. This makes it easier for your dog to understand what you want, as long as you're consistent in their use. The Stay means to "stay until I return to you." The Wait command means to "wait where you are until I give you a command to do something else." If you've studied the pictures of signals, you will also see that there's a small difference in the signals for each of the commands. We prefer that you use these signals along with the commands.

Stay—As you start to teach the Stay, your voice must convey a meaningful demand, not just a request. Practice a few times to see what tone is needed to get the best results, but don't bear down with a scolding or punishing tone. After giving the command, move out to the front of your dog, keeping control of your lead to prevent him from breaking his position, and repeat the command. Avoid looking down and glaring at him, because eye-to-eye contact can develop problems if continued. Repeat the command and gently shake the lead from side to side. If you see the slightest sign of movement, stop the shaking and gently raise the lead upward

HAND SIGNALS

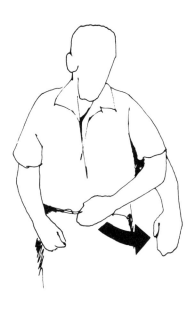

Fig. 6-6.   Stay.

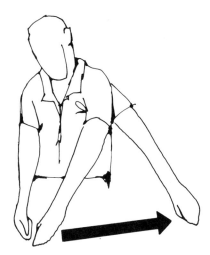

Fig. 6-7.   Wait.

as you give the command Sit, Stay. Shake it again, stop, repeat the Stay, and return to heel position. When you return to his side, keep control of the lead and go back slowly. Don't pull or jerk the lead as you move.

When you are back in the heel position, praise him for a job well done! This tells him that he has performed the correct way. Repeat this exercise three to five times before going on to something different, and continue for as many days as necessary, until you feel that he is responding well and understands the meaning of Stay. Use it during all of your regular practice sessions to keep it fresh in his mind.

If you are training your dog from a wheelchair, you'll have to leave him in position and move away from him before attempting the Stay. This means that your guide must be removed. If it will assist you more, obtain help from a friend who can work to the outside of your dog or who can go out in front of both you and your dog as a substitute handler.

When you return to your dog, if you are using a chair, crutches, or other aid, allow enough room as you circle around him so that he will not be frightened.

Wait—The Wait command might be more difficult, especially if you are using an aid. Don't start working on this until your dog has become steady on the Stay command. You must be careful and take it easy. Do not expect miracles, because the biggest stumbling block is trying to move ahead before your dog is ready. It pays to take a little extra time to teach an exercise that is going to benefit you greatly at a later time. This applies to any of the exercises. Be sure that the Stay command is being performed well (when you can go to the end of the lead and count to ten) before you start to teach the Wait.

When you have given the signal and the command to Wait, move forward slowly, keeping the lead loose. When about five feet away, turn and face your dog, call his name, and give the command Come, moving backward a short distance at the same time. Stop so that your hands are free to help guide him in to you. Praise him for coming to you on the command. Don't worry right now about getting him to sit. When moving backward, be sure that the lead does not tighten until after the Come command has been given, and then only if absolutely necessary.

Extend your distance on this recall very slowly. If you notice that your dog is moving toward you reluctantly, back up to the beginning to see if you can discover what has caused the slow-down. Perhaps it was a jerk on the lead and he thought that he was being corrected for *coming*. Work it out with him again, and don't forget the praise.

Fig. 6-8. In the recall exercise the dog should come and sit in front.

Come—When this is going along fine, it is time to start teaching the recall *in motion*. With your dog at heel position, give him the command and/or signal to heel, and move forward at a normal pace. Plan to work at different distances as you practice. Call his name, and as you get his attention, give the command Come and start moving backward. Try to increase your speed slightly as he turns toward you, encouraging him to come to you in a trot and showing no resentment. Make an effort to ensure happy work. Clap your hands, laugh, and make your voice pleasant. When you are sure that your dog knows what you want when you say Come, take advantage of every opportunity to use it and keep him used to it—don't let him forget.

Working on the Street

You have now taught your dog to stand, sit, heel, stay, wait, and come. As you continue your practice sessions, use all of these commands but mix up their order. Don't make your pattern the same day after day. This is boring for both you and your dog and can be a chief reason for your dog's lack of attention. And you *must* have his attention all through your training.

Now that you have your dog under fair control on lead (granting that there will always be room for improvement with more practice), let's change the scene and go out on the street for a workout.

Your first new exercise on the street is to teach your dog what he should do when you approach a curb, whether it be on a main street or a small side street. Always stop at a curb and teach your dog to either sit or stand, on command, so that you will have time to assess the traffic conditions and cross safely. When traffic is passing, reassure your dog by talking to him, letting him know that all is okay. When the way is clear, praise him and heel him as you proceed to the other side. Move down the street and practice another crossover. Soon your dog will automatically stand or sit as you slow up and stop at the curb. This is what you've been working toward, so pile on extra praise for a job well done.

Try crossing at an intersection where both directions of traffic are moving so that your dog can get used to congestion while he's stopped and while he's in motion. As you approach people, move slowly and let your voice reassure him. If he forges, remember to use your *body* to control the lead, passing it behind you. Be pleasant to strangers you meet, pass the time of day with them, and greet them with pleasant hellos. You will be pleasantly surprised to find out how this influences your dog's reaction to strangers.

Another move to give even more experience is to park yourself and your dog in front of a store where you can watch everyone pass by—people with shopping carts, dogs, children, bicycles, skateboards. Stay alert and try to control your dog without relying on a tight lead. Talk to him and teach him to be aware of these people, but don't let him become overly aggressive or too protective. Watch for the signs that will alert you, such as if he raises his hackles (hair on his neck and back), lays back his ears, or grumbles. If he is disturbed, take hold of his collar, talk to him, and calm him down. You might even find it necessary once in awhile to give a good sharp correction. It's better to take care of such a problem the first time it happens rather than let it repeat and worsen, thus becoming increasingly difficult to eliminate.

While you are moving along the sidewalk (if it's not too crowded), try weaving from one side to the other as people come toward you. In case you get a nasty look once in awhile, don't be disturbed by it, because you are working for a special purpose. Remember the old adage, "Sticks and stones may break my bones, but words (or looks, in this case) will never hurt me." Concentrate on the job of teaching your dog that it is perfectly normal for people to pass you on *either* side, regardless of their direction of travel.

Help him, too, in getting used to traffic noises and other associated sounds. The most severe reactions of your dog will probably come when he hears a siren, because the pitch is so high and a dog's hearing so sensitive that the sound actually hurts physically. If you hear a siren on an approaching vehicle, come to a halt, take hold of your dog's collar to prevent his lunging, calm him down, and reassure him with your tone of voice. When the noise has passed, give him a lot of praise and move on, *away* from the noise maker. Don't give him the idea that you are going to follow or chase the noise. And never overextend your practice sessions on the street, any more than your regular training exercises. Return home to rest *before* either of you become tired. Always stay alert and try to avoid trouble before it happens.

If you're in a wheelchair or are using a walker, replace the guide, including the flag, before taking your dog on the street. This is a precautionary measure and a reminder to your dog that you are still in control. You must be especially alert and ready to react as necessary, no matter what the situation. Using the guide will relieve you of the need to keep the lead tight and will keep your dog's confusion to a minimum.

Down

Now for the Down exercise—teaching your dog to lie down on command or signal. This will not be a miraculous, overnight affair, but it will be much easier than you may think provided that you put the necessary time into your practice following a complete demonstration to your dog of what you want him to do. He *must* be *shown,* and without force or harshness on your part.

You will accomplish more in a shorter time if you get down to your dog's level. Remember when you were teaching the Sit and the Stand to your puppy with no forward motion, just sitting down by him or squatting and working with the collar and your hands to show him what you wanted as you gave him the commands? You might have to change your position a bit, but be sure that you are comfortable. Understand what and how you're going to do an exercise before you start. Your dog will be sitting at Heel position, so be careful that your knee does not interfere with what you are doing. If he is tense and stiff, wondering what is going to happen to him, you must first get him to relax by reassuring him with your voice. Then pick up one front foot and shake it gently until you see it loose and floppy. Do the same with the other front foot. Next, reach over his shoulder and take hold of his front leg on that side. At the same time, take hold of the other leg with your other hand. As you are talking to him, raise both legs and bring him into a sitting up position. Keep him there a few moments until you feel him relax again. Tell him "G-o-o-o-d," give the command Down, and at the same time, slide his legs forward and down, applying slight pressure across his back with your forearm or wrist (depending on the size of your dog). Also, tip him toward you so that he will be comfortably on his side in the Down position. Keep him down for a few moments, praise him, and release him from the position before you repeat the process. Remember to let him know how pleased you are. Also, be sure to tip him toward you so that his legs are not underneath him. This will make it easier for him to be relaxed and steady.

Fig. 6-9. Starting to teach the down.

If your dog is large, you may have to vary your technique to make it easier for both of you. After you get him relaxed, take hold of his collar with one hand, place the other hand behind his front legs, and as you give the command Down, apply a little straight downward pressure, or tug on the collar and slide the front feet out and down to the desired position. If you feel tension building, such as if he is trying to lift his rear quarters and stand or is beginning to show resentment, give him an okay and get him back to a sitting position at your side. Start over and take it easy. Be patient with him, but get him to do the Down, then give him lots of praise.

Fig. 6-10. Only after accomplishing the Down at heel and in motion should the Down be tried while facing your dog, staying within controlling distance.

Once you have accomplished that first Down, each successive one will become easier. You'll know that you are beginning to reach your goal when he starts to respond to your command as you apply a little downward tug on his collar. However, don't take it for granted that his lesson has been learned at this point and see if he will go down on just your command. If he gets away with just one refusal, he's in control of *you,* and you will have to start all over again. Gradually ease the tension on the collar until you can take your hand off the collar as he's going down. As you remove your hand, put it in front of his head, palm toward the floor, and move it down with him as he goes into position. At the same time, give him another command to Down. Your hand should reach the floor when he does. Praise him lavishly, then release him from the position. This is the beginning of the hand signal that you will be able to substitute later for the voice command.

Try to progress by using just fingertip tension to start him down, then follow through with the signal and command. Then give the command, and if he doesn't start, repeat the command and use the signal at the same time. When he will go down on command and/or signal with no other aid, then and only then are you ready to work on lead in motion, while he is heeling at your side. However, don't hesitate to give him extra help whenever he seems unsure of himself or confused, or perhaps is just ornery.

When you start to practice the Down while heeling, be sure that your lead is attached to the non-working ring of the collar. Avoid any possibility of resentment in connection with the exercise. If you are physically able to bend down when you give the command, give the lead a little downward snap. Use a second, sharper command and a more effective snap on the collar if you find it necessary. This may seem like a correction to your dog, so don't put too much emphasis in your motion or voice. Don't give him any reason for disliking it.

Do this from a stationary position. Heel your dog forward just a short distance, then stop and give the command and/or signal. Repeat the command only once. And don't wait to see if he will do it. Follow through immediately with the reminder that you may need, but use it only if necessary.

Next, heel him forward and give the command and/or signal to Down while you are still in motion. Get the Down and stop at the same time. Remember the praise! Be careful how you give the command. Don't draw it out like a rubber band. Put authority in your voice, but don't make it sound like punishment. As you practice the Down, along with the rest of your lessons, be sure to include it in your changes of pace. Your dog should respond no matter how fast or slow you are moving. Make your practices interesting by putting in plenty of variety to avoid boredom. Be happy yourself, and keep it fun for your companion.

Chapter 7
FOR THE HANDICAPPED

As we observe life going on around us, we are more frequently seeing handicapped people of all ages making great efforts
to participate in activities usually indulged in by normally healthy
people. This is to be admired, and such determination is to be
envied by those of us who are blessed with good health. One of
the fields in which we are particularly interested is training a dog
for companionship and, in some cases, for actual competition in
shows. Naturally, the latter situation has limitations and must
conform to regulations set by a show-giving club. But this is not
our prime concern.

We are interested in helping handicapped people to basic
train the canine companion that they would love to own and
enjoy. It is quite possible with the proper approach and knowledge, a logical choice in a dog, a little help from a friend or teacher
at the beginning, and the use of a training aid.

In addition to the general advice and information given in
Chapter Two, still more factors enter into this special situation,
such as the individual's age and size, the extent of the handicap,
the necessity of grooming ease, and the dog's temperament, characteristics, and size.

We will try to cover as much material as we can, but it is
impossible to include every type of handicap. Therefore, we will
have to limit this to people who can conceivably attend some kind
of obedience training class or obtain help from an individual
instructor who understands the problem and is willing to help.
Check what is available in your area.

One group that we will not attempt to include is blind or
nearly blind people. This is because the field of training is very
specialized and should be handled only by those teachers with

proper experience. One of the best in the country, by the way, is the Guide Dog School for the Blind located at San Rafael, California. Its facilities and staff are of the highest quality.

If You Use a Walker on Wheels

Regardless of the walker style, you must first properly introduce your dog to this inanimate extension of you. The walker should be stationary, not rolling. It will be easier for you, too, if you enlist somebody's help to handle the dog. A good, reassuring tone of voice is necessary for both of you. Take your normal position in the walker and carry on a conversation with your helper as he or she is controlling your dog on lead. Be relaxed, and laugh and joke a bit to keep your dog relaxed, too. Let him sniff the walker and examine it as much as he wishes. If he is afraid to come close, have your friend bring him close, kneel down, and touch the walker, encouraging the dog and reassuring him that he has nothing to fear. This introduction will be the foundation for the rest of his training, so it's very important for your dog to not be afraid or confused by the walker.

If you have not already taught your dog the commands Sit, Stand, and Down in a stationary position, go back to Chapter Four and follow the instructions.

Your next step will be to reassure him that there is nothing to fear when the walker is in motion. Again, you'll need an assistant to help with the dog, walking beside you and the walker, practicing until you see that your dog is moving with confidence.

Pictured here is a guide that we designed to be attached to a walker or a wheelchair on either the left or right side as needed by the individual. It is adjustable to the size of the dog. This guide is only to teach your dog his proper position so that he will not forge, lag, or swing wide. Once he learns that position, the guide can be disassembled, one section at a time, until your dog needs no guide. It may become necessary to return to using it for awhile as a refresher.

Study the diagrams of the bracket guide and the pictures showing it in use. It can be attached to almost any place on a wheelchair or a walker, depending on the size of your dog and how tall he is. The adjustable arm can be lowered, raised, and even removed according to the problem at hand, causing your dog to correct himself. The lead threaded through the "eye" on the bracket is there to remind him that he is on lead and under control. The small flag is to alert people to exercise caution and not collide with the unit.

Fig. 7-1.
Bracket attached to walker.

Fig. 7-2.   Front section of guide bar, showing use of ring for leash to slide through.

CONSTRUCTION DIAGRAMS FOR GUIDE

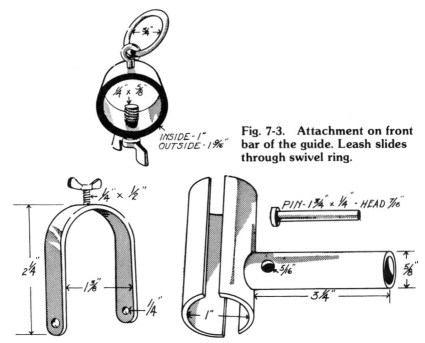

Fig. 7-3. Attachment on front
bar of the guide. Leash slides
through swivel ring.

Fig. 7-4. This piece attaches
the guide securely to the walker
or wheelchair.

Fig. 7-5. Piece that connects to
upright of wheelchair or walker
to hold the guide at the correct
height.

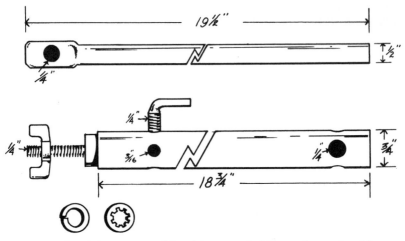

Fig. 7-6. Breakdown assembly of front and side sections of guide.

Attach the guide aid to the walker at such a height that the front bar is chest high to your dog. Adjust the outside section so that it angles downward slightly to prevent your dog from swinging outward, away from your walker. Fasten your lead on the dead ring of the collar, then tie it to the ring on the bar in front of your dog, allowing enough slack to let him sit down comfortably. Fasten the rest of the lead to the handrail behind your hand. This will get your dog accustomed to seeing the lead in the position in which it will be later when you're controlling him with it.

Your helper should have good timing and a good tone of voice, because he or she needs to have control of the dog as you move, relying only on a hand on the collar. No corrections, loud voice, or commands of No should be given, just guiding.

Now for a try. But first, give your dog a little refresher session of the exercises Sit, Stand, Wait, and Stay. Then with him in position in the guide and your helper ready beside him, call your dog's name and give him the command Heel as you move forward slowly. Your helper will guide him as necessary with a hand on his collar to keep him from ducking under or trying to jump over the guide. Just a few starts and stops for short distances should be all that's necessary. Vary your stops by alternating with a Stand, then a Sit. It's amazing to see how fast your dog will adjust to this arrangement as long as he has already learned some basic obedience. Be sure to praise your dog so that he understands what you want. If he sometimes moves well without needing an extra hand on his collar and you feel that you have his attention, then try the exercise without your helper.

Fig. 7-7. Arrows indicate possible locations for attaching the guide. Adjust height depending upon size of dog.

Be sure that the guide is attached properly and the lead is in place, then fasten the lead to the dead ring of the collar. Remember the importance of your voice for getting his attention. Call your dog's name and command him to Heel, and at the same time, start your feet in motion to propel yourself forward slowly, using no more motion of your legs and feet than necessary. As soon as your dog is moving, encourage him with your magic praise word of "G-o-o-o-d!" After a few steps, as you come to a halt (not after you have stopped), give him the command to Stand or Sit. Use your voice for praise at this point rather than physical contact with your hand to avoid any exuberance that might result in his jumping against you or the walker or getting tangled in his lead.

When you've both gained confidence and your dog is moving steadily (and by this time you are probably tired of going in a straight line), try making some turns to vary your practice routine. Make your first turn so that the walker will be moving away from your dog (left side, turn to right; right side, turn to left). Think ahead about what you will be doing so that you will know how to move your feet. As you start the turn, call his name for attention and keep talking to him as you slowly make the turn, keeping a smile on your face. When you make the opposite turn, be even more careful, and do plenty of talking so that he won't shy away from you or the walker. Remember that your dog is well aware that you are responsible for whatever the walker does, so don't make any mistakes with it that can possibly be avoided. Otherwise, you can expect a setback in training. Always keep your dog's attention and get him to slow down or hesitate just before you start the turn to allow yourself time to manipulate the walker. Your turning just ahead of him will cue him as to your intended direction.

When you have become more or less proficient in making both turns, you can change this movement and extend it into circling to the left and to the right, bringing variety into your heeling practice and making it more fun as well as practical. Ready to give it a try?

Start as usual, and when both of you are going along smoothly, speak his name and start your first circle, turning away from your dog. Complete the circle, then go straight again in the same direction in which you were moving before the circle. Maintain your speed and rhythm as you turn. Don't try any sharp moves or pivoting, as you will confuse your dog and keep him from moving normally. Make your first circles rather large, decreasing their size gradually.

Enjoy this new exercise and let him know how much fun it is. When you're moving well again in a straight line, try the circle toward your dog. Make the circle fairly large at first, and be careful not to bump into your dog. When you feel that he's responding well to your voice control and to the lead tied to the ring on the guide in front of him, you may attempt the about turn.

The about turn can be a bit tricky but should pose no problem as long as you do the circles well in both directions and use common sense. Remember to call your dog by name to get his attention just before you start to make the turn, and be careful of your timing. Make all your about turns away from your dog. When you have gone half a circle, head straight in the opposite direction.

Your next heeling exercise will be changing pace. In order for you to be prepared to adjust to different situations in your daily life, you should be able to change to a very slow or fast pace and still have your dog by your side with no extra effort. In practicing, change smoothly from one pace to another, talk to your dog, and use his name to keep his attention.

When you have perfected (as nearly as possible) all of the exercises and changes, you need to get your dog used to working on a completely loose lead, depending solely on your commands, praise, and conversation, before you eliminate the guide. So far, the lead has been tied into the guide ring. Now you will just pass it through the ring, then anchor it near your hand, as before. Don't loosen the lead so much that it hangs down and gets in your dog's way. Now go through your practice sessions and include your turns, circles, about turns, and changes of pace. Don't be impatient—everything worthwhile takes time, and you and your dog will be a better team for it and will understand and appreciate each other more every day you work and play together.

When you can do all of these exercises to your satisfaction on the loose lead, you can remove the first section of the guide. This is the arm that extends backward along the far side of your dog. His heeling pattern should be well enough established so that he will remain in the proper position and won't swing away from the walker. If you find that he is not ready, replace the section and work with it in position for a few more days. Keep the lead passed through the ring, sliding free, as long as the front section is still in place. Use a little pressure against the lead as needed when you must get his attention and let him know that *you* are in control during your practice sessions.

If you're quite sure of yourself and want to make your next step, please remember that this is a most important one. It involves the removal of the next section of the guide: the bar that extends in front of your dog.

Before taking it off, work your dog for a few minutes with it in place, then allow him to watch its removal. Give him the command to Sit and Stay or Wait, and keep him under control with the lead. When the piece is off and out of the way, you may want to change the fastening point of the lead to the opposite side of the walker, bringing it across behind you so that your body will absorb any unexpected sudden pull, as in forging. Always be prepared for some unforeseen action. You don't want to risk having your walker pulled over or jerked away from you.

Get yourself and your dog into position, and adjust your lead so that your dog can walk in the position to which he is accustomed. Ready to move? Call his name and give the command to Heel as you move forward. Go only five or six steps, then halt and have him Sit. Remember your magic word to use for praise. Make any further adjustments that may be necessary before moving again. Take it easy as you repeat the different exercises, and don't try to do everything in one session. Do not hesitate to replace any or all parts of the guide whenever you feel that your dog needs the extra help and a reminder of his proper position.

The first time that you take a walk where you might meet people and where they might be overtaking and passing you, go back to using the complete attached guide, including the flag. Be ready to do your share of getting out of their way, because some people won't bother to move for you. And you always encounter a smart aleck who thinks that it is cute to tease you, annoy you, and even tease your dog. Play it safe. Move to the side and ignore them as much as possible, and keep from getting both yourself and your dog upset. Remember to be patient and use common sense, and you can avoid most unpleasant incidents.

If You Use a Walker Without Wheels

You will find some differences in getting your dog used to the more jerky or irregular forward motion of the walker without wheels. However, the same training procedure should be followed. Your timing of commands as you start the training will become even more important, depending upon the ease and rhythm of your forward motion and the amount of hesitation needed between each forward move.

Before working with your dog, you must first do some practicing with the guide attached to the walker. This will get you accustomed to the new experience of feeling a change in the balance and weight of the walker. As you get ready to move it, concentrate on offsetting the change in balance and be ready to compensate for the difference. Then think about how far that first move of the walker is going to be. Keep your balance as you move it ahead, and move into it again. As you must already know, your handling of it gives almost a rocking motion. You don't progress in a smooth, flowing pace. You rock the walker toward yourself before lifting it ahead. Be sure to keep this raising of the front legs of the walker at a minimum to avoid jerking the lead on the dog's collar, as he may interpret this as a correction, especially if he is a small dog. This will also avoid bringing the front bar on the guide

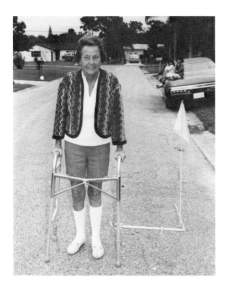

Fig. 7-8. **Practice using walker and guide without the dog.**

up in front of the smaller dog's eyes. You may even find that running the lead through the ring on the bar, instead of fastening it, will make it easier in some individual cases. As you move, set the walker on its rear legs and let it down as it rocks from you. It then takes your weight. Naturally, the going will be easier on a floor or sidewalk than on the ground, so adjust to the surface accordingly.

Practice handling the walker with the guide attached, trying to perfect your timing and smooth control and working in as straight a line as you can. Be sure that you have the necessary confidence in using your walker before you try handling your dog at the same time.

Introduce your dog to the walker just as with the other type. It may be necessary to spend more time and use more caution as you first introduce him to the motion due to the distinct kind of rhythm—rock, move, set it, hesitate, and repeat. If you can enlist the aid of another person, it will help greatly and save time.

When you position your dog, allow enough lead from his collar to where you tie it into the ring on the guide in front of him so that his collar will not be jerked when you start to move forward. Your timing of commands is critical, because your dog must

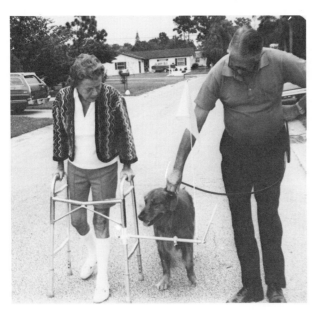

Fig. 7-9.
Assistant
guides dog from
outer side.

be alerted and commanded just *before* the walker is moved. At first, with your helper controlling your dog with his collar, just rock the walker back and forth a few times before moving it to let your dog get used to the motion beside him. When he doesn't seem to mind it, give the commands and take your first step. Let us add one command to help your dog. It will go like this: Name (for attention), Stand (as you get ready), Wait (as you rock the walker toward you), Heel (as you lift it and move forward), and Sit (as you stop). Your timing will depend not only on the size and action of your dog, but also on the span of each move of the walker and your own speed in moving.

When you think that you are ready to try without an assistant, be very careful, and *do* take it slowly until you are sure of both yourself and your dog. Don't be too anxious to detach sections of the guide. Be patient with your dog, and remember that he doesn't learn any faster than you teach him, nor does he learn any more than you teach him. So train him slowly. He will let you know when you're going too fast for him if you pay attention and learn to *read him*. It is up to you to develop him into a true companion, one that will stand by you and help you to the best of his ability.

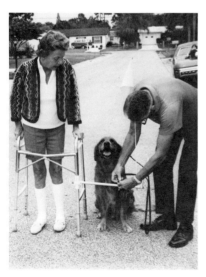

Fig. 7-10. Assistant fastens dog in position.

Fig. 7-11. Walker guide properly adjusted for large dog.

If You Use Crutches

Now for a few comments if you use any style of crutches (the typical underarm, the shorter type with the forearm cuffs, or the four-point quad cane). None of these will prevent you from training a dog to be your well-behaved, obedient companion.

Again, as with the walkers, your timing and expertise in handling the crutches or quad cane are critical in accomplishing your goal. If it's necessary to use the guide, first practice handling the crutch with at least the front bar attached, keeping in mind that the movement must be as smooth as possible. Be careful to avoid swinging the crutch outward, where your dog will be heeling.

When you start working with your dog, fasten the lead across the rear of your body at your waist level to a part of your clothing, such as your belt, in such a way that it doesn't slide. This way, the shock of a sudden lunge by your dog will be absorbed by your body. This is a preventive precaution, since a dog's behavior can be unpredictable, especially under unusual circumstances. In all other aspects, follow the instructions step-by-step as they are given for those using walkers.

Fig. 7-12.   Try to keep dog in heel position while practicing "Figure 8" turns.

You probably will have to teach yourself a modified pattern in making your turns, remembering to practice first the turn *away* from your dog. Just as in regular heeling, make a special effort to keep your feet away from in front of the dog. Otherwise, his progress will be blocked and he will lag. Concentrate not only on getting your feet out of his way, but also on getting the crutch out of his way. As soon as he understands what you want and gets used to it, he will make his own adjustments.

In turning to the right, put your weight on the right crutch and use it as the pivot point. Then use the left crutch to turn and propel yourself forward. Move the crutch out of your dog's way as quickly as possible. Reverse the procedure for the left turn, still being careful to get the crutch and leg out of your dog's way. Always think of the motion from your dog's point of view. The movement of your crutch will cue your dog as to your direction of travel.

For the about turn, work as above, but when you turn make a half-circle before you start forward again, heading in the opposite direction. Take it easy, because you have double the distance to maneuver in the turn. Be particularly careful to keep your crutch from swinging out in front of your companion, "threatening" him and making him lag or shy away from you. Practice handling the crutches because keeping your balance is the key to your success in training your dog and obtaining his confidence and love. His trust in you is worth all of your efforts in training him correctly.

If You Use a Wheelchair

Next we will concentrate on helping those who must be confined to a wheelchair, whether it is moved by your hands on the wheels or by motor. Because dogs are very sensitive to motion, you may face special problems with certain dogs, but not all of them. The introduction to the chair must be made slowly and cautiously to eliminate the chance of frightening your companion.

As you can see, the training guide is designed so that it can be attached to any one of several different locations on either the left or right side of the chair. The side on which it is used will be determined by the individual. The guide serves the same purpose as already detailed for use on the walker. It teaches your dog his proper position when moving alongside you and the chair. Just as on the walker, it can be adjusted according to the size of your dog.

Because your dog has never had to stay next to a large, moving wheel, this introduction should take place *before* any training is attempted. To lessen the distraction of this movement, we suggest making a plain circular cover with elastic through a hem on the outer edge. The cover should be just large enough to fit over the handrail of the wheel. Or maybe you can come up with an even better idea. The purpose of it is to cover up the sight of the moving spokes, which could confuse your dog and take his mind off the training. It can always be removed later when he's at ease and is working beside you with no problems.

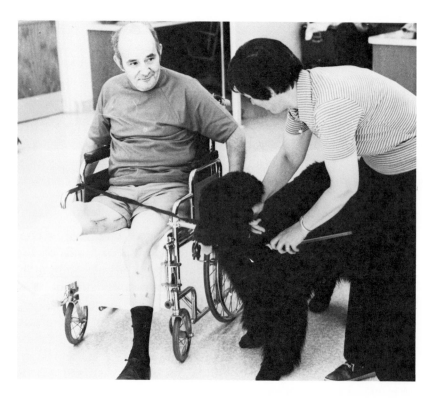

Fig. 7-13.   Dog and guide in correct position with wheelchair.

When you introduce your dog to the guide, follow the same approach as with the walker. Have someone help you control your dog with the collar as you begin to teach him his position when you are in the chair. If you think that you will not need the weight of your body against the lead later on, just fasten the lead to the arm of the chair on the side where your dog is working. Remember: the lead is first fastened to the ring on the section of the guide in front of your dog.

When you're ready to move forward, remember your commands. Talk to your dog and praise him, and *do not* see how far you can go. Your goal is to teach him the various commands needed for good performance, obedience, companionship, and trust in you with no fear of your wheelchair. You must be patient and content to go slowly. His training is also done for your own safety, because you certainly don't want him to do anything that might interfere with the operation of your chair.

When your dog is responding well to the Heel command and is staying in position and standing or sitting on your command as you come to a halt, the next step is to teach him to remain at Heel position when you turn the chair to the left or right. It would be wise to practice this with the guide attached, but without your dog at first.

When making the right turn, hold the right wheel so that there is little forward motion, and rotate the left wheel, making the right wheel a pivot point for the turn. When the chair reaches the proper position, rotate both wheels together to get a smooth forward motion. In your mind, picture your dog's position and think what his reactions might be. Practice.

Follow the same procedure in reverse for the left turn, remembering to hold the wheel on the inside of the turn stationary as you rotate the outside wheel to the proper position before you move forward. Regardless of which side your dog will be working on, practice first the turn *away* from that side. Control the tone of your voice and remember to watch the timing of your commands and the movement of your chair. Give plenty of praise. When turning, be ready to give extra encouragement to keep your dog up in Heel position, because this could start a bad habit of lagging and might lead to worse problems.

When you turn toward your dog, keep the wheel on your dog's side steady until you've made the turn and are ready to move forward. Give the Heel command as you go. Teach him that he must hesitate long enough to allow you to turn the chair and not bump into him.

As you practice the about turn, it may be easier for both you and your dog if you make the turn away from him. Again, watch your timing, your tone of voice, the movement of your chair, and the position of your dog. Always remember to praise. And be sure that you can do all of the turns and changes in speed with ease before you remove any sections of the guide.

If you are interested in show competition, the American Kennel Club does allow entries using wheelchairs. However, the regulations require your dog to do all of his heeling on the left side, the same as the regular entries. This means that you must decide what you want to do before you start your training. Study hard and be sure that you understand the rules.

Work on improving your turns, because they are critical for the smooth and rhythmic motion of your dog. Follow instructions for teaching all the other exercises and commands, praising, and correcting only when necessary. We wish you the best of luck.

Chapter 8
TRAINING TO
HELP THE DEAF

We have already seen how versatile the training of a dog can be, depending upon the understanding the trainer has of the individual dog and the purpose for which the dog is being trained. We have covered training for companionship, good canine citizenship, general good behavior, basic control for hunting and other utilitarian purposes, and training for people who have various types of physical handicaps, chiefly those that make it necessary to use wheelchairs, crutches, walkers, and other aids.

It takes people with VERY special training to work with dogs that are being taught to lead the blind. And the dogs that are selected are the cream of the crop in intelligence, disposition, and personality. We admire the dogs and their instructors and put them at the top of our list. In general, these dogs are purebred and registered, most of them being German Shepherds, Labradors, Golden Retrievers, Doberman Pinschers, and Smooth Collies.

A program is now developing along the same line that gives hope to dogs in animal shelters and dog pounds. Selected dogs are being trained to be the ears for those who have impaired hearing or no hearing at all. Regardless of whether they are purebred or crossbred, if they are medium to small in size, healthy and strong, and good-natured, loving, attentive, and intelligent, they can be candidates for training in this special program. If you're interested, contact Hearing Dog, Inc., in Henderson, Colorado.

We will endeavor to instruct you in some of the ways to train your dog to help you with your hearing impairment. For these exercises you will not have to depend upon the services of a specialized trainer. Besides, you can begin immediately once you have your dog and do not have to wait your turn to obtain a dog trained by the Hearing Dog Program.

In a few areas, training clubs have incorporated special classes for this type of training. Because "signers" are necessary for instructing the deaf in a class, volunteers are recruited to assist regular instructors in communicating. We were privileged to observe a class (Handi-Dogs, Inc.) in Tucson, Arizona, composed of deaf people training their own dogs. Each person was assigned a volunteer from the club, as well as a "signer," who interpreted the instructor's directions. We helped them and other handicapped members at a seminar, giving them additional ideas to further their progress. The club is to be congratulated for its worthwhile civic effort.

Training your own dog can be fun, interesting, and rewarding. But a word of caution: as in all training, don't expect too much of your friend and protector, and don't push him too far too fast or you will get absolutely nowhere, and nobody will enjoy what they are doing.

Before you begin, we are assuming that you have already read the preceding chapters in this book, because the general text is directed to all phases of training and helps you to develop special rapport between you and your dog that is necessary before you can "specialize." If you have not read, studied, and practiced what you found in the first several chapters, *go back and do it right now.* Don't try to put the cart before the horse.

First, let us go over a few points for consideration for those of you who still need to choose your dog. It is preferable for you to select a small or medium dog. The reason for this is simple. When he has been trained to let you know that a bell is ringing, someone is knocking at the door, or the baby is crying, he jumps up on you to get attention, then leads you to the origin of the sound. And who wants a St. Bernard, Irish Wolfhound, or Newfoundland pouncing on top of him? In addition to not wanting a large dog to jump on you, think about whether you have a large enough area for him to exercise. The bigger the dog, the more room he'll need. Also consider your own capability to handle and control a large dog.

Review thoroughly the chapter "Choosing the Right One" and think of all the pros and cons—purebred versus mixed, male or female, long coat or short, and color. Of prime importance is the temperament of your dog. You don't want a timid, cowardly dog, nor do you want an aggressive, fighter type. He should be a happy medium, able to think for himself, not easily frightened, quick to learn, and, of course, love to play. You also should consider having your female spayed or your male altered, at the advice of your veterinarian, to avoid difficulties that could arise later.

We will not be dictating any rules that will change your way of life, but you must realize that you will be making adjustments when you add a little canine character to your family that will become your friend as well as your ears. You must learn to respect each other and to read him from his reactions, expressions, and movements. Try to put yourself in his place, get down to *his* level to look at the different situations that develop. Give him lots of love and affection, for he will give you all that he has without being taught. He already does that on his own. Learn how best to get your teaching across to him so that it will be easier for him to learn.

When you start your basic obedience training, which will be the foundation of the special training, develop good control, dog attention, and a desire on his part to do things willingly to please you. Remember to always train humanely and give lots of praise, and you will have an easier and more enjoyable time as you grow together. The loyalty and pleasure will be immeasurable for both of you. It is a balanced give-and-take project. Loyalty cannot be bought or forced; it must come from the heart to be true and dependable.

If you are still unsure of yourself and your training and feel that you need more help, try to locate an obedience training class that will allow you to observe the work, even if a training fee is required. Judge for yourself if you want to imitate the methods used. See if both the humans and the canines are happy and enjoying themselves. For now, limit your observation to the puppy, beginner, and novice classes. Later you may want to watch some of the advanced training. Don't let yourself be influenced by any force methods to achieve quick results, for those results are not the happy and willing type of work that you are seeking.

Before you begin any special training, your dog should be under good control and giving you attention, as well as responding to the commands Heel, Come, Down, Sit, Stay, Wait, Stand, Hup (or Over or Jump), Go, Speak, and Quiet. Then you will be able to use these commands, as well as several others, in training your dog to be a useful companion as well as your newly acquired ears no matter where you might be.

You already have the recommended basic equipment, but you'll need to add several items to this list, depending upon the number of situations you will be training your dog to respond to. Some of these items are:

- alarm clock
- whistling tea kettle
- electric doorbell and buzzer
- whistle
- smoke alarm with light
- sound tape of a baby crying
- two metal door knockers
- rolled up newspaper
- short length of soft cotton rope, three knots near one end
- old wallet, key case with keys, eyeglass case, etc.
- old glove, slipper
- metal key ring with keys.

Should you wish to introduce one of the new exercises into your regular training for variety, it will help keep both of you from being bored. Introduce it first so that it will seem more like a game, and your dog will catch on fast. You get more serious later.

Additional exercises can be taught to your dog to increase his usefulness to you in your daily life by helping you to overcome many difficulties caused by your hearing loss. The choices are yours to make, depending upon your needs. Follow the training instructions very carefully. Be very diligent, generous in showing your appreciation, and learn to view all your work from your dog's point of view. Be understanding!

Here is a list of exercises:

- alert you for the front door
- alert you for the back door
- alert you for a ringing alarm
- alert you for a burglar alarm

Fig. 8-1. All hearing dogs are trained to respond to a knock at the door.

- alert you for the smoke alarm
- alert you for a baby crying
- alert you for the buzzing of a stove timer
- alert you for water or food boiling over
- alert you for burning cigarettes
- alert you for someone calling to you
- alert you for TV trouble, set left on
- teach your dog to ask for food, water
- teach him to pick up dropped objects
- teach him to find lost articles.

As you see, all of these exercises pertain to situations within your home, except for the last two, and they can apply outdoors when you are playing or taking a walk with your dog.

Add to these the following that are special for outside activities:

- riding on the elevator to arrive outdoors
- training to exercise at curb or specific areas
- heeling for sidewalk walking
- learning caution at street crossings
- teach ignoring other animals (no chasing)
- alerting for sirens, horns, whistles
- alerting for leaving your car motor running.

First, a few general notes before we get into specific exercises. If your plans call for working alone, you can probably get a lot of help by using a cassette tape that has sounds to which you wish your dog to alert you. Be careful not to confuse your dog. For instance, if the tape is sounding a knocking on a door and you open the door, the tape should not continue the "knocking." Keep your training periods short, and do not repeat one exercise more than three to five times before changing to a different one. Make all of it interesting and fun. You're not training to compete at a show. It is for your own pleasure and the help that you want from your dog, so make your own rules. Learn to read your dog, and he will let you know if he feels like working. Some days he'll be ready to work much longer than other days. His enthusiasm for the training sessions can fluctuate, as well as his stamina, just as ours changes according to our mental and physical state. If you think that you can improve your approach to the training so that he'll enjoy it more and get more out of it, take the time to study what you're doing, then try out ideas to see if they work better. Teaching your dog to play ball with you, having him retrieve it, take it, hold it, and ask you for attention to continue the play will also help you in some exercises.

Take, Hold, and Pull

The commands Take, Hold, and Pull can be taught using a short rope with knots on one end. This is not, as you'll see, a game of "tug-of-war." You may have to taunt your dog a bit with the rope at first to get him to take hold of it. After all, this is a new item, and it feels quite like a ball in his mouth. But he must learn to take it and hold it when you tell him to. When he gets used to it, he'll start to pull on it. Encourage this, but don't exert pressure on it yourself. Move and go with him in any direction he wants. Do not make the mistake of trying to yank it away from him. Squat down to his level, call him to you, assure him that everything is okay, and tell him to Give. If he doesn't cooperate immediately, run your hand down the rope until you touch his mouth. He will then release it as you keep repeating the command. Give him praise, for both of you have accomplished much. This exercise will be gradually changed to tugging on your clothing or pulling you by the hand.

Alerting for Inanimate Sounds

The next exercise is teaching your dog to jump up on you. This will be another way for him to tell you that something is happening that needs your attention. Avoid, to the best of your ability, a forceful jump against you or his landing on top of you if you should be sitting or lying down. Avoid harsh corrections, however, because any kind of alert is better than none at all, especially if your life might be in danger. If you find him getting onto the furniture just to enjoy the comfort of it, when you're not occupying the space, then he should be corrected. Don't punish in this case, merely speak his name and give the command Off in a harsh tone. Praise him and smile as he obeys. Off is a good word to teach for this command because he is not likely to confuse it with others. Keep his command words as simple as possible, and he will learn them more easily.

If you can arrange ahead to have someone knock on your door at a certain time, prepare for it by having your dog on lead. When you see him alert to the knock, place his front feet up on you, then walk toward the door, making him think that he is leading you to the sound. Don't move out ahead of him— encourage *him* to lead out. Use a command, too, like Show Me.

Fig. 8-2. The dog then finds his deaf master (in this case the trainer), and leads him to the location of the knock.

Open the door, greet the knocker, and praise your dog for another job well done. Naturally, he will not learn this in one lesson. You will have to repeat it many times before it registers completely, but don't be impatient, and don't let him become bored with it.

Study the construction diagrams of how to install knockers, bells, and buzzers for the special use of you and your dog. You will notice that a light bulb is incorporated into the warning box. This makes it easier for you to tell at a glance which door is to be answered after your dog has alerted you. Metal knockers are fine, but when used on both doors, they probably would create the same sound, and your dog could become quite confused. If you use them, try to get some that do not sound the same.

Fig. 8-3. Dog and trainer arrive at the door.

When you think that he is getting the idea and is alerting you with the expected reaction on lead with no additional help from you, then you may try a few times off lead. Keep the lead handy in case you need to return to it, even though you only use it as a reminder once in awhile. Do not expect your dog to realize immediately which door he is to go to. It may take some time, but don't be surprised if he starts to lead you in the right direction very early in the training. He may be able to do a lot more than you had originally thought. He will give you reason to brag about the other half of your "team" long before you have any idea of what he can do.

When your dog hears a new sound in your home, you must be alert and ready to investigate when his actions tell you. Be ready to follow in the direction he leads you, telling him Show Me, Take Me to It, Where Is It?, or some similar command. These are different from the usual obedience commands, but he will know what you mean by them. Some of these sounds, very important to you, might be a kettle boiling over on the stove, a timer set for something cooking, or a faucet that you forget to turn off.

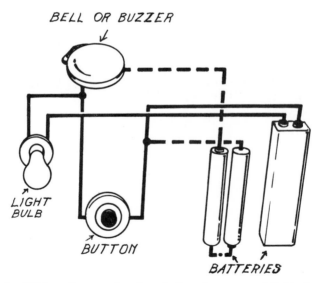

Fig. 8-4. **Wiring diagram for door bell or buzzer and light. A separate set is needed for each door. Battery size is determined by power required by bell and/or light.**

He should also learn to alert you when your wake-up alarm rings. This one is easy for you because you get to lie down and relax while your dog does the work. Just be sure that you only pretend to be sleeping, because you can't direct him if you are really asleep! Set the alarm for a short rest period, and let him wander on his own in another part of the house. Watch the time so that you can tell when the alarm is supposed to ring (you'll be able to tell, of course, by feeling the vibrations). If he should come in on his own, don't let him see that you are awake. If the sound fails to bring him in, call him and get him to jump up on you. Then praise him and shut off the alarm.

You can train for this even at night, after you have gone to bed. You can put the alarm clock under your pillow so that the vibration will waken you if you go to sleep. Take the clock out and place it on the nearby table or chair as it continues to ring. Call your dog, get the alerting signal from him (jumping up on you), then shut off the alarm and give him lots of praise and loving. By planning lessons and following through, both of you can enjoy

Fig. 8-5.   Hearing dog learns to wake his sleeping master.

each other and have fun. At the same time, your dog will be developing into a wonderful pal and useful helper.

To train your dog to alert to a timer used in preparing food, use the same procedure as with the alarm clock. Set the timer in connection with something that you are doing in the kitchen so he will associate the area with that particular sound. Sit down to eat or read, or occupy yourself in some manner, keeping an eye on the clock so that you'll know when the timer will sound. Watch your dog for any sign indicating that he hears a sound, such as a change in position of his ears or his moving. Call him and get him to jump up on you, asking him, What Is It? or Show It to Me. Praise him, then follow him to the kitchen, shut off the timer, praise him again, and even reward him with a biscuit if you wish to let him know how pleased you are. Be careful about using food as a reward, however, because frequent use may give him the wrong idea, and he may go into his alerting act for no reason except to get a tidbit. And you surely want to avoid behavior like that!

Smoke alarms have their own peculiar sirenlike sounds, and many are built with a lamp bulb that lights. When your dog alerts you to this sound, all you need to confirm the reason for it is to look for the light on the ceiling fixture. With a burglar alarm, all lights should go on throughout the house. Proper installation can take care of this.

You also need to encourage your dog to search and find you in order to give the alert, no matter where you are in the house. Use the alarm clock, because he is already familiar with the sound. Set it while your dog is somewhere else, and be sure that your wristwatch agrees with the clock so that you will know when it is supposed to ring. Go into another room to hide. If he hasn't found you when it is time for the clock to be ringing, start calling his name and be sure that he finds you—don't go to him. And don't make his finding you easy. When he does reach you, get him to alert by jumping on you. Praise him, then run to shut off the alarm, giving him a little excitement and letting him know that you are pleased. Don't play this game too often or he will start playing sharpy and will not let you out of his sight.

Fig. 8-6.   Another method of teaching a dog to alert, this time to the telephone ringing.

Alerting for Human Sounds

The next exercise may take some doing, and you may need to get assistance from someone who has a tape recorder and can make a special cassette for your use. Also, it applies only to certain people: those who need to know if the baby is crying. You need a cassette player (usually made for both recording and playing and reasonable in price). You may even find a place where you can buy such a tape already recorded. If not, have the crying made according to the way you want it—long cries or short—but loud enough so that your dog has no trouble hearing it. Be sure that a space is left between the cries so that they sound natural. After all, even a crying baby has to catch his breath once in awhile.

Begin the training on lead and go off lead when you find that your dog is beginning to understand what he's to do. Return to using the lead if you deem it necessary. You may wish to start with a doll in the crib at first, since the cassette in the crib may disturb a real baby. Be sure that the first ten minutes of the cassette are silence, before the crying starts. This creates a more natural situation and allows you to get to another section of the house. Keep track of the time, as in previous training, so that you are ready to observe your dog when he hears the baby. Encourage him to lead you to the "problem area," then have him jump up on you as you approach the door of the bedroom where the crib and the crying are located. Praise your happy helper, go to the crib and soothe the "crying baby," and turn off the tape. You can revise this procedure to meet your own particular needs, but always depend upon your dog to let you know if you're going too fast or are expecting too much from him. Use him as your guide, and he will come through for you much better than you expect if you give him the understanding and appreciation he deserves. Always train any new exercise on lead at the beginning, and do not try anything off lead until you're fairly certain that your dog understands what you want him to do. Return to on lead whenever he seems confused and work that way until the problem is resolved.

When you do go off lead, watch very closely as the preset time approaches for any alerting signs exhibited by your dog. Get him to jump up on you *before* you start to move this time. Praise him and tell him Show Me or whatever words you are using, run into the room with the crib, and complete the lesson as before. If you are using a real baby, quiet the baby before returning him to the crib or carry the baby out with you. Let your little alerter sniff the baby if he wishes, and tell him that he belongs to the baby, too!

Training for the next exercise should begin indoors, and, when mastered, it should continue to the outdoors. Again, you need the cooperation of a second party, such as a friend or neighbor. This activity involves teaching your dog to alert you to someone calling you. Accurate timing and planning are important so that you will know when to watch your dog and read him for alerting signs. Later, you can accompany the voice call with the already learned knock or buzzer, but one thing at a time. Decide whether you want to try it at first off lead.

Fig. 8-7. A dog can be trained to alert a hearing impaired mother to the cries of her infant.

Fig. 8-8.   The dog leads the trainer to the "crying" baby.

At a prearranged time and with you in a room away from the door, have your friend open the door and call your name. Your name should already be familiar to him, and he should realize that you're wanted so that he will come to you with no difficulty, alert you, and lead you to the door. Give him plenty of praise, then follow him and greet your friend at the door. After this exercise has been learned, set up an outdooor situation. You could be playing with your pal in the backyard and someone could call you from the front gate, the porch, or the front door. The possibilities are numerous. Approach each situation the same way.

Retrieving

Another practical exercise for use both inside and outside your home is teaching your dog to retrieve any article you may have dropped. Because your own hearing is impaired, this could conceivably happen easily, and without the help of your dog's keen ears and his ability to find and retrieve, you might lose something important to you.

Retrieving (even a ball in play, but on command) is very important and will now be put to practical use. To begin, do some short retrieves of an article (a glove, key case, or other object) just to have fun, but use the same article for awhile because you want to associate your scent with it. A leather glove is ideal at first because it holds scent well and is comfortable in your dog's mouth.

After a few retrieves, move to another room without your dog and drop the object behind a chair or other piece of furniture so that your dog won't see it when you call him. Make a fuss, and tell him that you lost your glove. Let him smell your hand so that he will associate it with your asking his help to find the glove, but don't hold your hand over his nose. This only fills his nose with your scent, and, until his nose clears, everything that he smells will smell like your scent. Teach a command for this exercise and be consistent, always using the same word for the same job you want done. Some suggestions are Find It, Search, Look for It, Find Mine.

If he seems confused at first, slowly move in the direction where you dropped the glove, watching him as you go and repeating the command. Then make a big fuss over him as he finds and retrieves the glove. This will become a new game and a challenge for him, and you'll both enjoy it. Vary the drop and the times, carrying the glove as you work around the house doing your regular chores. Don't try to fool him, however, or make it impossible for him to make the find, even though he becomes proficient and works enthusiastically to find each drop. Remember the famous Aesop's fable of the little boy who cried "Wolf" once too often, and learn from it.

When you think that he is ready for it, change from the glove to a key case. He should learn that he's supposed to pick up and retrieve anything that you have dropped or lost. Repeat the work with the key case, using the command until he will pick up the key case for you on his own, without a command. Next, use the case

Fig. 8-9. Dog is taught to notice when trainer drops items.

with one key hanging outside so that he gets used to having metal touch his mouth or be in his mouth. Another aid to get him used to the feel of metal (some dogs cannot stand it) is to give him an occasional tidbit of a favorite food on a spoon.

Continue with the key case until several keys are hanging outside. Then work with other articles, such as a wallet, a change purse, an eyeglass holder, a date book, or a rolled up newspaper. You'll be surprised how your dog will love to work for you and how he will do it all for praise and your showing your appreciation. This gives you a good idea of what your dog can learn if you teach with understanding, love, and patience.

Fig. 8-10.   Dog returns lost item to trainer.

You can later transfer this same training to the outdoors. Make sure that you do your training on lead, unless you are fortunate enough to have a fenced yard. Drop the articles in different places, as you did in the house. When you think that you can depend upon him, start practicing as you take your walks along the sidewalk. Have confidence in your dog and watch him. He may surprise you and want to turn back because you have accidentally dropped something and were not aware of it. Follow him where he leads you, giving him the benefit of the doubt. If he is right, go overboard with your praise. That's what this is all about. Don't correct him for turning back, even though his reason may have been an error this time.

Working on the Street

Street control and attention on you, as well as awareness to everything around him and a readiness to alert you, is of great importance to you. So let us start from the beginning of a typical walk with your dog and point out what you should do as well as how you should train your dog for future help from him, regardless of the type or degree of your handicap.

With your dog on lead, open the door and go through it, and, as you close and lock it, have him sit until you're ready to take off. Then give him the command to Heel and keep him in the proper position. If you have stairs to go down, keep him at your side. Never allow him to bolt ahead of you going down or up the stairs. If you see that he needs to relieve himself, first take him to the proper area, and, once that is taken care of, have him return to your side and remain in the proper Heel position. Also remember to clean up after your dog before leaving the area. It is your responsibility as a dog owner. If you find that he still wants to sniff around, give him a little sharp correction with the lead to remind him that he has a job to do as your companion and protector. You are his "special charge," and he should not be allowed to forget it, nor should he be expected to do his work without appreciation from you.

As you come to a street crossing, always halt and have your dog Sit or Stand-Stay (depending upon the weather), then give an

OK, Heel, or whatever command you want to use when you are sure that the way is clear in all directions. If you realize that a car is coming one way, look in the opposite direction and give an OK. As he starts to move, snug the lead, and as the car goes by, reach over and praise your dog for waiting. Soon he will realize that he must make decisions himself, that your OK does not always indicate that it is safe to proceed. He should learn that at any crossing, he should Stop, Look, and Listen.

It is extremely important for your dog to alert you to sirens, because you cannot always see from which direction they are coming. There might be an ambulance, a police car, or a fire truck just around the corner from you. And if they are answering a call, they are NOT going to slow up much at a crossing. You must be warned that such a vehicle is near. Usually the pitch of a siren hurts a dog's ears, and he'll set up a howl. This you can easily see and respond to. Teach your dog to stop in his tracks and refuse to move until all danger has passed. If you have a fire hall, police station, or hospital near you, you are lucky because you can train (with lead on, of course) under real conditions. If you do not, enlist the services of a friend and a tape recorder with a tape of sirens. Avoid any voice association with these sounds. Communicate by signs, by touch from your friend, by a lettered card held up for you to see, or some other nonverbal method. You want your dog to react and stop at the sound of the siren. If other people may be on the sidewalk, just step off to the side to avoid interfering with them. As always, remember the praise.

Your next lesson is to teach proper behavior and control in case he meets other dogs, cats, or other small animals such as squirrels while you are out on your walk. It is only a natural instinct that prompts your dog to investigate other dogs and communicate with them. We don't know what they say or how, but we certainly can tell a lot by their actions—and sometimes it's more argument than casual remarks! It's also instinctual for them to run after animals like squirrels and rabbits, or maybe even to go on "point" if they see or smell a bird. All these are interesting distractions, and unless your dog is under your control completely and is paying no attention to them, he is not working for *you*. Being dragged at the end of a lead in front of a car or truck is not exactly the picture of what a Hearing Helper is supposed to embody.

If you see such a distraction, just step to one side with your dog, watch the traffic or the people go by, or look in a store window—but keep your dog's attention on you. *You* should be his first concern. Make sure that he recognizes this, no matter what the distraction.

If You Forget to Turn Off Your Car Engine

A number of people who are deaf, wear hearing aids, or have only partially impaired hearing drive autos, and some might forget to turn off the engine in their cars before leaving them. This not only can be dangerous, it is also illegal and a temptation to car thieves. If your dog is taught to alert you, this can be avoided. You can train your dog to alert you to this situation by having him jump up on you and return to the car to tell you that something is wrong. Work on lead and go only a short distance from the car before you ask him to alert you. Return to the car and have him put his front feet up on it. Open the car door, take the keys out of the ignition, and heap on the praise. Don't worry about a little toenail scratch, because it is more like a badge of honor for saving your car. It is more important to have a car that needs a paint job than to have no car at all!

Final Reminders

As we wind up this section, let us reiterate a list of what you should keep uppermost in your mind as you train:

- don't overtrain
- don't expect miracles
- don't depend upon corrections
- don't consume alcoholic drinks while training
- don't train when you are overtired
- don't mistreat your dog; be humane
- vary your exercises, mix them up
- go slow and easy, work one exercise at a time
- don't use harsh corrections; think
- love your pal, as he loves you.

Chapter 9
HELP FOR THE NON-VOCAL DEAF

As everyone realizes, helping someone who is doubly handicapped becomes extremely difficult unless that person is already trained in sign language. But this should not prohibit such a person from owning a dog, loving it, and training it to be a companion and helper. We have seen excellent results, proving that it can be done if the person is patient and understanding and has the necessary "stick-to-itiveness."

Let us give you one example. A young woman and her husband attended a problem clinic that we held several years ago for a training club in New Jersey. They had a female Airedale named "Belle" that had been trained enough to get her C.D. (Companion Dog) title from the American Kennel Club. The club to which this young woman belonged had helped her, and she had taught her dog to work completely on hand signals, taking her directions from the judge in the ring by lipreading. Her husband also helped her in her training since his hearing was very impaired but was not completely gone.

She had the determination to go on to train for advanced competition, and her dog was all heart and full of understanding, responding to her every need. At this point, her therapist advised her to try voice commands in her training because it would be excellent practice for her. Of course, her commands were very guttural in sound and the enunciation was poor, BUT her dog understood what she wanted! The final outcome of this woman's determination was that she finished two more titles on her Belle, that of C.D.X. (Companion Dog Excellent) and U.D. (Utility Dog)! You see, it can be done, and if you approach your training with the understanding and patience that your dog deserves, you can do any of the exercises that your pattern of living and wishes dictate.

Nor do you have to participate in formal competition in order to prove what you and your friend are capable of accomplishing.

Now to get to some special help for you. Remember that the training is done the same in all the basic work, as already covered in the text, and your dog can be taught to Heel on whichever side is more comfortable for you, unless you might want to enter formal competition with a purebred registered dog, and then, of course, heeling must be done at your left side.

It is especially important for you to study your pal and be able to read him from his facial expressions, the tipping of his ears, his body motions, and other signs in order to understand his reactions to yourself and to what you are doing when you are with him.

Because your dog is blessed with a keen sense of hearing, sounds will be very important to him, regardless of what they sound like to hearing humans. And first in importance is the call name. Choose a name that is fairly easy for you to enunciate and that will be different from the regular commands you will be using. Remember—the name is used to get the dog's attention and is given along with the command for the job to be done. Following are phonetic sounds not used in usual commands that may help you choose a name that begins with one of these sounds: ad, an, as, ab, ack, art, ba, bud, ben, bro, bus, blu, ed, ess, ell, em, en, in, il, jo, jan, jim, june, lar, lem, lo, les, my, mel, meg, mat, nan, nel, net, nat, pam, pet, pol, rap, ron, rus, tex, tad, tan, tam, tug, van, ves, vor, yen, yin, zane, zone. Find a sound that is easy for you to say, then choose or make up a call name that begins with this sound, emphasizing the first letter. If you have a purebred and wish to register him with the American Kennel Club, the call name does not have to be part of the registration name. However, if you wish, you can choose part of the formal name as the call name, such as "Prince Valiant's Johnathan" might answer to "Jon."

Practice saying your dog's name and accompany it with pleasantries, smiling, hand clapping, and much praise. He will soon realize that this particular sound refers to him, and he'll learn to respond to it. Say his name with a smile and be consistent every time you repeat it. Be sure to praise him when he comes to you as you say his name, even though you haven't started to teach him the command Come. A reward of a tidbit would not be amiss here, as long as this does not continue as a regular routine. Associate your voice with his more pleasant experiences, such as when he's eating, playing, or going out for a walk or ride. This will counteract any fear he may have had at the beginning on account of your voice tones.

In addition to the regular training equipment, we ask you to get three more items: a narrow-mouthed plastic whistle, a metal "cricket" (makes a clicking sound), and a cassette tape recorder. Enlist the help of a friend to record many of the sounds around your domicile—sounds to which your dog should become accustomed, such as your laugh, humming, your voice as you do your chores, the rattle of pots and pans, the noise of a vacuum cleaner, doors opening and closing, and the telephone ringing—but never use your dog's name. You will be using the whistle to help call your dog to you from a distance. And the cricket noise clicker will help to control your dog in certain situations and parts of exercises without drawing attention to yourself, especially if you're heeling your dog near a crowd. (If you cannot locate a "cricket," another soundmaker be substituted.)

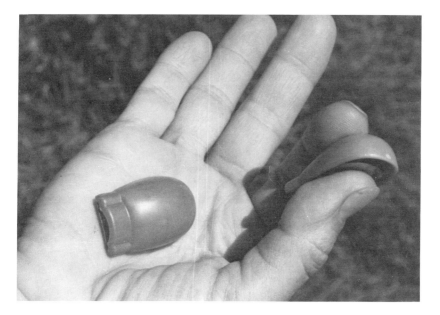

Fig. 9-1.   Cricket clickers that can be used to que a dog.

Anyone with a handicap has nothing of which to be ashamed, but it's only human nature for any of us to be conscientious about drawing the attention of others to our own frailties and abnormalities, no matter what they may be. If we can avoid such situations, we feel more secure and self-satisfied. Naturally, if you are thinking ahead to a possibility of earning some obedience titles, none of these extra aids are allowed in competition in the show ring.

Learning to say the commands that you teach your dog may call for special help from a therapist, especially when it is necessary to distinguish between similar-sounding words such as Sit, Stay, and Stand. We will list here the most frequently used commands, and it will be up to you to practice and get as close as you can to the correct sound, remembering, again, to emphasize the first letter of the word. The commands are: Heel, Come, Sit, Stay, Stand, Down, Wait, Go, OK, Show Me. Take it slow and teach the meaning of each to your pal, as described in the earlier chapters. Be particularly careful on consistent pronunciation of the words. Be sure to keep your dog on lead while training. Before you start your sessions, practice saying the various commands in combination with your dog's name, always using the name first to get his attention. Be sure of yourself and the command words before you start working because you don't want to risk having a confused dog.

As you proceed with your training as described in the other chapters, take it slow, be patient, and be guided by your dog's reactions and expressions. Don't press forward if a problem develops; back up in your training until you iron it out. You may also find it necessary to use a signal with a command at different times. This is why we advise you to obtain the whistle and the "cricket."

Combining these with your commands may seem complicated when you first think about it, but take it step by step and you'll see how easy it really is. The whistle is to be used with teaching the Sit and the Recall. Use a short, single blast with the Sit command and a trebling of the whistle for the Come (recall). When your dog fully understands this association, he will respond to both exercises on just the whistle. Ask a friend or family member to help you if necessary in ascertaining your progress in mastering the treble for the recall. It is done chiefly by your tongue, along with breath control.

The "cricket" is used particularly for outdoors when you are in crowded areas, such as in pedestrian traffic on the sidewalk or a shopping plaza parking lot where you don't want to draw attention to yourself. Teach your dog to respond to this new sound in a location where you can command with your verbal signals at the same time with few or no distractions. Each time you tell him to Sit, use a single click, and as you start out with the Heel command, make it a series of clicks. He will soon be responding to the clicks without the commands.

Continue advancing in your training as your dog displays that he is ready for it. Get him to alert you to different sounds and situations, traffic at street crossings, sirens, and anything dictated by your own needs. It is necessary for you and your dog to be able to communicate, and this can only be achieved through patience, understanding, logic, and much love and praise.

Once you and your dog have mastered the basic exercises for everyday living, you will have built the firm foundation that is required for any other special duties that you wish to teach or any advanced training that you might fancy. (If you are interested in formal obedience competition, refer to one of the books listed under Suggested Readings.)

Regardless of what you teach your dog, you and he will do it together, as a team, and you'll continue to enjoy each other and have fun as you go. Be proud of what you accomplish in spite of the handicap, and be ready to show the world! Never forget to let your pal know how much you appreciate him, for after all, he's your partner and a member of your family, and his loyalty cannot be bought.

Chapter 10
TAKE, HOLD, CARRY, AND BRING

One activity that is both practical and that can lead to more fun and play with your companion is teaching your dog to pick up objects and bring them to you. Again, in order to accomplish this without resentment and to keep the training enjoyable, it must be done in slow and easy steps. In other words, as a baby learns to creep before he walks, your dog must learn to take and hold an article before he carries it and brings it back to you.

But even before these steps, he needs to get used to the feel of your fingers against his lips and teeth and in his mouth without resenting it. This can be very easy, especially if you have had your dog since he was a puppy, or even if you got him as an older dog and he is blessed with a good disposition. If you have a problem with resentment, do not force your dog with inhumane methods such as pinching or twisting his ear to get him to open his mouth, using a pinch collar, putting force on his mouth, or other such tactics that only worsen the situation.

To introduce him to the feel of your fingers, get yourself and your dog in a comfortable position where both of you can relax, such as on the davenport (provided you allow your dog on the furniture), in a chair, on a hassock, or even on the floor. The easiest way for you to control your dog as you work with him is to have him sit with his back toward you and tie the lead to your leg (dead ring of collar). Make the lead just short enough to keep your dog under control and allow you free use of both hands.

Get your dog used to the feeling of your fingers on his lips and against his teeth by using either hand. Control him by placing your other hand in the collar in case he tries to turn his head away. If this doesn't work, just put your other hand alongside his head so that he can't turn it. The main point is to get him to accept holding your fingers in his mouth without creating resentment. Don't overdo it and get your pal all frustrated. Keep him calm by talking in a good tone of voice.

If your dog gives you serious trouble, such as showing complete resentment to the point of trying to bite you, laying his ears back, or showing fright in his eyes, he may need a severe correction before you can accomplish anything. This severe correction does no damage, and its success lies in the element of surprise, depending upon your timing. Be sure that he's in a controlled position, such as facing away from you and sitting between your knees. When he shows resentment, hold his collar with one hand and come up under his jaw sharply with the fingers of your other hand, palm up. Make the impact hard enough for him to feel it and be surprised by it. Gauge the severity of the slap by the size of your dog. A smaller dog needs only a tap, and a toy dog usually requires only a flip of your thumb. Always consider your dog *before* you do anything like this. And another must—praise should follow any correction *immediately,* just as it should follow any approved performance. If at any time you lose control of yourself or show your temper, stop immediately before it's too late. You cannot say "I'm sorry" to him and have him understand why. Just stop your training *before* you have a reason to be sorry. Resume it later when you are composed and have mended your ways.

When you can touch his teeth and he doesn't resent it, you have passed the big hurdle. Control him with the collar or with pressure of your knees and gently work one finger into his mouth as you teach the command Take It. Accompany this with the soothing words Easy, Easy. As you remove your finger, teach the command Give or Out, or whatever you choose, and give plenty of praise for his fine cooperation. Remember to be positive when giving commands; mean what you say. Demand, don't ask, but make your demand pleasant.

If your dog clamps down on your finger from pure resentment, you may have been pressuring him to go too fast. Patience, *very* short periods of training, and lots of praise and pleasantness will help you here. You must gain his complete trust before trying to continue with the training. Never use force to open his mouth.

Talk to him and get him to relax, and he will soon open his mouth and will enjoy your praise.

Your next step is what we refer to as "threading the needle." You will need three or four different sizes of plastic straws—the small cocktail size, the kind you use for a thick malted drink, and about three-eighths inch and one-half inch diameter pieces of plastic tubing, sold by aquarium or laboratory equipment supply stores.

Put your dog in the same position as before, in which you have complete control. Refresh his memory by touching his teeth and praising him. Take the smallest straw and show it to him so that he realizes it is nothing to fear. Even rub it against his face, keeping it in his view, so that he can feel it. When he relaxes, bring the straw to the side of his mouth, touch his lips with it, raise his lips with one finger, and put the straw against his teeth. Talk to him all the time, saying Take It. Slowly move the straw back and forth until you find the space between the upper and lower teeth, then rotate the straw toward the front as you gradually push it farther into his mouth. Remember the Take It command as you work. He will very likely open his mouth now, so be ready to receive the straw as you say Give. Be sure to praise him. He was just reacting normally and starting to spit it out as it pushed against his tongue, but you have turned it into a command performance! Easy?

Next time he will relax sooner, take the straw easier, and hold it a few seconds. But be sure to continue its rotation. Let him adjust his tongue to be comfortable before you ask him to give it to you. He is now trying to please you and is looking for the praise that he knows is on its way. Soon you'll be able to "thread the needle" all the way through to the other side of his mouth, but be careful that the straw doesn't push against the inside of the lip as it emerges. Raise the lip so that the straw will have free passage all the way. Tell him how great he is, make a big fuss over his accomplishment, count to five and say Give, receive the straw and really lay on the praise. Repeat this no more than five times and no less than three for one training session. If you wish to plan two or three practices in one day, it is fine, provided you use caution and don't overdo it. Don't take any chances of overtiring your pal and building resentment. He has hardly started on the first steps.

When he starts to open his mouth as the straw touches his teeth, introduce the straw at the front of his mouth. To make this easier, hold the straw so that your forefinger is free. As you bring it toward his mouth, first touch his lip with the finger, then press it against his teeth, saying Take It. He knows the command and is already used to your finger on his lips and against his teeth, so the only new change is coming from the front instead of the side. As he opens his mouth, slip the straw in just behind the canine teeth. He can carry it most comfortably at that position, *not* toward the back of his mouth, regardless of whether he has an "even bite," a "scissor bite," or is "overshot" or "undershot." Don't shove the straw toward the back because this may start a bad habit of his chewing and mouthing anything that you put in his mouth.

As you progress to using a straw or piece of tubing with a larger diameter, it is much easier to find that special spot for it to rest. Right now it's especially important for the object to be small so as not to become a distraction to him. As you practice, stop assisting with your finger as soon as possible. However, be ready to depend on it whenever necessary. When you can touch the front of his mouth and he will open it on your command and take the straw, then you are ready to try the next step—working with a wooden dowel.

Due to the fact that some dogs dislike the wood surface and try to spit it out, we're going to back up and first present a small-diameter dowel like the small plastic straw. Start the same way as before and thread the needle with it. Follow the same procedure until you feel him relax as he takes it and holds it, then work from the front of his mouth, being careful where you place the dowel and remembering to use the proper commands and lots of praise.

At this point, you should check your dog's mouth for the proper size dowel, that is, the diameter which is most comfortable for him to hold. (Eventually this information will be used in making a dumbbell, but for now we still have much to do with just the dowel before working on retrieving.) With a selection of dowels slightly different in diameter (sometimes one-sixteenth inch larger or smaller can make a difference), place one in the proper place behind the canine teeth. Holding his mouth closed over it, but not tight, tap what protrudes of the dowel on either side of his mouth. You can tell easily if it is too loose—what we refer to as a sloppy fit. The dowel might be too small, or it might be too large. The only way to find out is to try other sizes. You'll know when you get to the right size because your dog will let you know that he likes that one best! If you're testing a puppy, be prepared to test him again when he has matured, because his mouth and teeth will very likely change as he grows.

With the right size dowel to work with now, repeat the previous lessons to the point of his holding the dowel to a count of fifteen. Use all of the commands that you have been teaching. Receive the dowel on command and give lots of praise. Then go through the same steps, but this time give your dog a Stand Stay command before you present him with the dowel. Again, work up to where he will hold it for a count of fifteen.

When he responds to the Take It from in front, you're ready to gradually increase the time of the Hold command. He must hold the dowel without help from you, so start by gently releasing any pressure from your hands. If he does it, great, but don't see how long he will do it before dropping it! This is a step-by-step process, and you must be patient. If he should tip his head down, bring it back up and place one finger under his chin, repeating the Hold command. Practice until you can see that he's holding without your help; *not* necessarily in one session.

When he will hold the dowel to about the count of five, start forming the habit of bringing your hands up from underneath it to receive it as you say Give. Don't take hold of it and pull, because this will hurt his teeth and make him dislike the whole idea. If he likes to hold it that much, just exert a slight pressure forward

Fig. 10-1.
Presenting the
dowel.

(from the back of the dowel), give him the command, and he'll release the dowel to you. Then really give lots of praise. He will soon learn what the various commands mean and will cooperate as long as you're consistent and don't expect too much from him too fast. Repeat this exercise as often as is practical and convenient for you, gradually extending the holding time until you count to fifteen slowly. Make it easy and pleasant for him from the beginning, rather than teach him with force because you want to prove that *you* are the master. It's simply a matter of choosing between a dog that performs happily and because he wants to please you or one that performs as commanded because he's afraid of what may happen to him if he does not! Need we say more?

Now, for the first time, you will introduce motion into the exercise, which is the beginning of the Carry. This is why you worked the last step from the Stand, because it is the natural position for a dog. In addition, he doesn't have to think about moving from the Sit to the Stand. He's likely to drop the dowel or spit it out as he changes his position, so we eliminate that problem by starting from the Stand.

Give him the dowel and tell him to Hold It and Wait as you take two or three steps forward. Turn toward him, calling his name and telling him Come. Hold your hands out toward him and encourage him to you, reinforcing the Hold It so that he doesn't drop the dowel, and receive it immediately. Don't wait for him to sit first. If he drops it, do not get upset. Just return to Heel position, give the dowel to him again, and go through the same steps. Be sure that you don't go too far away. Stay within controlling distance so that you can reach out to prevent his dropping the dowel as he starts to move. Even help him to keep his head up, lessening his tendency to let the dowel fall out of his mouth and showing him what you want. The first time that he moves and holds the dowel until you receive it, go overboard with the praise. After this, you may start to increase the distance, but *very* slowly, keeping it fun, like a big game. If he should start dropping it again, you probably are moving too fast and need to back up to the first steps in the exercise.

When he comes to you from a distance of about twenty feet, add a hesitation count before the recall command, gradually extending the count from about five to twenty. The Take, Hold, Carry, and Give by this time should be well set in his mind as far as a dowel is concerned. Your next step will be to get him to repeat the exercise with a different article—a soft leather glove appropriate in size to the size of your dog. Prepare it first by taping the fingers together or tying them so that they will not flop around, looking like something alive with which to play. Also, roll and tape or tie the wrist so that the glove is more compact to fit into his mouth easily.

This may be his first taste and feel of leather in his mouth, so be on your toes as you start again on the Take and Hold. Don't allow him to start chewing it or playing with it. This is not to be treated like a toy—it is a work project, even though it should be enjoyable to both of you.

After you have progressed as far as you did with the dowel, you may want to add still more variety to your training. Different objects that you can teach your dog to hold and carry to you include: a key case, a wallet, a small basket, a slipper, a shoe, a purse, a cigarette pack, a rolled up newspaper, a hat, a small package, a glove (fingers loosened from having been taped), or a wooden dumbbell. When are we going to start teaching your companion to go out and pick up any of these items on his own, on your command, and bring them back to you? Just as soon as he's steady and dependable with carrying and holding and delivering to your hand on command. Right now? OK!

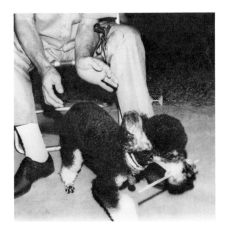

Fig. 10-2. Learning to carry the dowel.

We will begin with the wooden dumbbell, mainly because we can tailor it to be comfortable for him to carry as he's learning. This way he will have a pleasant association with the exercise. Be prepared to work on this step-by-step; don't try any shortcuts.

Now for the measurements to make the dumbbell—or give them to somebody else who can make the dumbbell for you. You already have the diameter of the dowel for the mouthpiece. To find out how far off the floor or ground this should be so that your dog's underjaw or nose don't scrape and get hurt, take the measurement from the top of the *lower* canine tooth to the *bottom* of his jaw and add one-fourth inch. The ends of the dumbbell should be twice this measurement plus the diameter of the dowel so that the mouthpiece will have ample clearance for your dog to pick it up. The length of the dowel between the ends should be long enough so that the ends do not press against the lips or a whiskery muzzle. Usually a one-half inch space on each side of the lips or whiskers is ample. Regarding the shape of the ends, we prefer those that taper from the dowel side outward, because they give any dog much better vision and, as a result, more confidence in what he is doing. A dumbbell fitted this way is carried level. It is easier because the dumbbell does not dangle on account of a mouthpiece that is too long, and your dog cannot pick it up by the ends because the tapered angle makes it difficult for him to hold onto the ends. Once your dog has learned to retrieve the dumbbell, you can teach him to bring other objects to you on command by applying the same procedures.

He already knows the meaning of the words Take, Hold, and Carry. Now we're going to present the dumbbell to him in motion, after you have introduced it to him so that it won't seem like something new. Controlling the lead with one hand, start heeling forward slowly, and with the other hand present the dumbbell in front of his mouth with the Take It command. Don't stop your forward motion; get him to take it as you are both moving. If he hesitates, press it slightly against his mouth and get him to take it and Hold It. Move on a few steps, then back up a few steps, call him, and receive the dumbbell with *lots* of praise!

Soon you'll see him starting to reach for it, depending upon how well you have taught him the basic command of Take It. This is a very important goal for you to reach in this series of steps. Let him know how pleased you are! Once he starts to reach, don't test him to find out how far he will reach, or you will set him back in your training. Keep him working happily, changing your pace and working to get a reliable performance. When you feel you've reached this point, you will be ready to teach him to pick up the dumbbell.

To begin, you should sit on a stool, hassock, or something similar, and have near you a box, stool, or something that is about chest high to your dog. Position it to one side of you, but keep it within reach of the hand that you've been using for the dumbbell. Your dog should be on the other side where you can reach his collar or control him with the lead up close to the collar. First introduce your dog to the box. Pat it with your hand and let him investigate it.

Now get him back in position and get your dumbbell. Hold it five or six inches away from his mouth and command, Take It. Guide him to the dumbbell if necessary, but get him to take it. Start again the same way, but this time hold the dumbbell just a little above the front edge of the box and guide your dog to it, again commanding Take It. Don't help him by bringing it toward him. See to it that *he goes to the dumbbell.* Practice this until he will go to it and take it from your hand by himself on your command.

The next step is to rest the dumbbell on the box near the front edge, keeping your hand by it as though you're going to pick it up. On the command, guide him a bit if necessary to bring him up to where he can reach for the dumbbell. Praise and encourage him as he tries to get it, and as he picks it up, call his name, causing him to turn toward you. Receive the dumbbell and praise him to the skies. Repeat the exercise and try to get him to pick up the dumbbell without your hand being on it. When he'll do this with no problem, you are ready to substitute a slightly lower box or object from which to work. You can continue, as your dog is ready for it (some grasp this faster than others), until you're actually down to floor level.

When your dog is picking up from the floor, within that short controlling distance, you may try some retrieves, no farther away than the distance at which you have been working. First, slide the dumbbell out this distance and give the command at the same time, combining motion and action. Keep his attention and interest. Help him if he needs it, but do not start trying for distance. Work an increase *very* slowly and gradually, up to around twenty feet. When he's reliable at this distance, start teaching him to retrieve other articles using the same procedure. Don't be afraid to back up your training if you run into any problems, and *do* keep it fun!

Chapter 11
TRICKS AND GAMES

No family unit exists successfully and happily on work alone. Some kind of balance is needed to bring enjoyment and fun into the overall picture, a break from serious concentration on training. As a child develops and learns through both work and play, so does a dog. And as a child increases his love of life, and family relationships deepen and strengthen via these channels, so does a dog improve his performances and increase his love for his master. Additionally, the whole family has more fun when a dog will entertain them and their guests with antics and tricks on command. For this reason, we are including some basic advice to help you accomplish these objectives.

Some of the basic commands that you've already taught your dog will come into use here, especially the Stay, Take, Hold, Come, and Out commands.

Shake Hands

We'll start with a simple one—Shake Hands, or Give Me Your Paw. Set yourself up so that you're near your dog's level (floor, hassock, low chair), and have him face you in a Sit position. Hold his collar at the back of his head and give your command as you gently tap behind one front foot with the other hand. Then pick up his foot and shake it easily. Restrain him if necessary with the collar, taking some of the weight off his feet. Laugh and talk to him as you go along. Release his paw so that he can put it back in position, and let go of his collar as you give him lots of praise. Don't worry if he breaks from the Sit position; you're not being too strict here. Just repeat the procedure the next time as you and he get ready for it. Soon he will get the idea and begin to respond to your request when you touch behind his paw. Each time he gives any indication of doing more "on his own," go overboard with the praise.

Give him variety by working on another one or two tricks, but don't confuse him with too many at one time. Always be consistent with your commands, and be sure to use the same words for the same trick. Don't make the mistake of changing them, even though they mean the same in *your* vocabulary.

Fig. 11-1. With a little work, your dog will learn to offer his paw for a friendly handshake.

Roll Over

After your dog has learned to respond to the Down command, the Roll Over trick is easy to teach. After he lies down and is on his side, help roll him over with your hands, giving the command and going through a circling motion with one hand where he can see it. Praise him and help him to go back again to the other side, using the new command and the circling signal. Release him with an OK, let him jump up and have fun, and give him oodles of praise. As he progresses, you'll find him responding to either the command or the circle signal and very willing to show off for you. Some will need more help and time than others, so be guided by your dog's response and work accordingly. Encourage him to do the trick on his own. Soon you'll find that you can even control which way he is going to turn by which way you start your circling signal. Be patient and have fun as you play together.

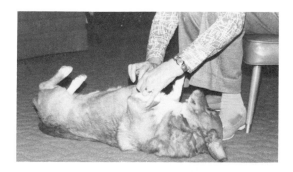

Fig. 11-2. Teaching "roll over."

Fig. 11-3. Directing the dog to stay in position after rolling.

Say Your Prayers

Another interesting stunt is to teach your dog to "say his prayers." The commands of Sit and Stay, already learned, are most useful in teaching this trick. Get your dog to sit in front of something on which he can put his front paws, such as your lap, a chair seat, or a bench. We have even seen dogs perform by sitting on a chair, facing the back of it and placing the paws on the back. But don't take a chance on anything that is not solid and stable. Be sure to use the phrase Say Your Prayers as you have him go through the motions, because this is what you're teaching him to respond to. Encourage him to rest his chin on his paws, and push his head down gently to let him know what you want. Hold it for a count of five, then release and praise him. Don't repeat it so much that he begins to resent it. Let him rest or go to something else after three or four tries, and always let him know what a terrific job he's doing. Once he gets the idea, he will enjoy the performance and the applause and will hold the pose longer for you.

Remember: in teaching *any* tricks, remove the help that you are giving him with your hands as early as possible. Don't lead him into thinking that he will always have you to help him. Get him away from this physical contact and teach him to be independent.

Fig. 11-4. Teaching "say your prayers."

Use extra gestures as needed and repeat your commands, for you are not restricted by any rules and regulations. You can even reward him by giving him a special tidbit for a beautiful performance. I used to get one of our dogs to do a trick for a piece of dog biscuit and would ask him to "pay for it." Just remember to be patient and take it slow. This is one place where you can really let your imagination run riot.

Sit Up

Another trick you can teach is to Sit Up. With some dogs it comes easier than for others. I almost ran out of patience with a Cocker Spaniel that we had many years ago. I was sure that his spine was made of jelly—no backbone in it—for that was the way he responded, even when I would put him into a corner of the room for extra support. I would hold him up and dangle a treat above his nose to direct his attention upward. Eventually, he found out that he could stiffen his back sufficiently to remain in position for a few seconds without my assistance. Then came a really laughable situation. I would tell him to Sit Up and show him the treat, and he would hunt around the room for an empty corner, go into it, and sit up! And when he realized that he didn't need the corner anymore, he behaved like a baby who had just discovered that he could walk by himself. He was proud as punch. And so were we! He just loved to show off by sitting up by himself out in the middle of the room.

The keys to teaching all your tricks are showing, praising, repeating, associating new command words, progressing slowly, withdrawing physical help as early as possible, and being enthusiastic. Dogs will surprise you with how fast they learn to do what pleases you and elicits applause. There's a little "ham" in all of them, and you may even find them inventing tricks of their own. Don't hesitate to capitalize on the situation if it should happen.

Play Dead

A natural follow-up to the Roll Over is to Play Dead Dog, beginning with the already important command of Down, Stay. When he's down, get your dog to lie on his side or on his back with all four feet in the air. With your hands, gently get him to relax and put his head down, using the Stay command along with the new

Dead Dog. Then release him with an Okay and lots of praise. Increase the time gradually and take your hand away as early as possible, but don't expect too long a stay in the position too soon.

Speak

Teaching a dog to Speak (bark) on command can become very useful and practical at a later time, in addition to being a trick just for entertainment. This usually can be developed by observing your dog's efforts to communicate with you. He might be disturbed by some noise or commotion that he doesn't understand, perhaps he's hungry or thirsty, or maybe he wants to go outside. He may let you know by a growl, a whine, or bark, or by jumping up excitedly. Be quick to encourage him to do more, and say Speak, or Talk To Me. Generate a lot of excitement, bark with him a bit if you're getting him to speak for food, and reward him with his supper and much praise as soon as you get a sound out of him. At one time, when we had two house dogs, I had one of them Speak for his supper and the other Whisper for his. Truthfully, I came up with the Whisper idea to protect my own sanity, for that one's bark was so shrill that I felt it was splitting my eardrums! Timing is all important here.

Praise for stopping the barking is also of value, again on a specific command. Never correct your dog for barking at suspicious noises, strangers at your door, or unusual situations. He is reverting to natural instincts to warn his family of potential danger, and this is one of the reasons why you want your dog for a companion. He does *not* need attack training to protect you.

Once he is responding to the Speak command, use it only when you have a real reason. Associate it with different things according to your own desires and needs such as the doorbell ringing, an auto horn blowing, the telephone ringing, or your dog asking to go out or to have a drink of water. Always praise him as soon as he Speaks on his own.

Refusing Food from Strangers

This project may take you longer to perfect, but it could pay off some day by saving your dog's life. It is teaching him to refuse food from strangers or picking up an object from the ground that may have been dropped or deliberately thrown into the yard to poison him. It's hard for us to realize that such cranks and psychos exist, but they do. Fortunately, the majority of people love animals, just as we do.

The first step in teaching this is to limit his accepting food, letting it come from one member of the family—the one who is most likely to be home regularly. Give the food only after a Speak command, always in the same dish, and with an OK release as it's put down for him. When preparing the food, once in awhile (*not* often), drop a piece on the floor by mistake. If he goes for it, immediately say Nein or Sit or Down in a firm, scolding voice to keep him from picking it up. Remove it from the floor and get it out of sight. Then praise him for being such a good fellow! Lay down your rules in your house and see that no one else feeds the dog—and no snacks or tidbits between meals. It's hard to follow these restrictions, especially when children are around, but it will be worth it.

If you're snacking in the evening while watching TV or enjoying company, have somebody drop food on the floor "accidentally on purpose." Immediately come in and give the same command as when you dropped food while fixing your dog's supper. Follow through the same way—pick it up and get it out of sight, praising your dog for *not* getting it.

When the "in house" training is well along, it's time to move outside and onto the street. To set this up properly, you will need the cooperation of a friend. Ask him to take a (preplanned) walk and drop two pieces of food that your dog particularly likes on the sidewalk. Have him space the pieces well apart, about thirty to fifty feet. If any wind is discernible, try to plan your approach so that the wind blows the scent of the food toward your dog. He'll be interested *before* he gets there, making it easier for you to read his reactions and prepare for the properly timed correction that *must* be administered if the training is to be effective. Make your approach nonchalant so that your dog doesn't suspect your planned move, but be ready to respond quickly. Act immediately when your dog begins to tip his head toward the tempting tidbit. Make the correction an effective snap and release, but do not repeat it. Give lots of praise, regardless of whether you had to give the correction. Repeat this lesson a few times until you feel that he understands his wrongdoing in reaching for something on the

floor or ground. Later you will be putting him through other similar sessions in advanced training, but you'll be doing it off lead.
Therefore, you want to be sure that he remembers. It *could* save
his life.

Make it a habit all through your training sessions to finish with
some fun with your companion, a sort of reward for him to antici-
pate. Remember the old adage, "All work and no play makes Jack
a dull dog (boy)." He likes a certain amount of play, just as a child
does, and loves you more for it. Use your imagination with your
fun and games and apply the obedience commands that he
already knows, thus reinforcing them in his mind while still having
fun. Both of you can enjoy such activities.

Hide and Seek

Playing a game of Hide and Seek can be started in a very
simple way by your ducking behind a piece of furniture in another
room, then calling your dog to find you. Don't overdo it to the
point that he does not trust you out of his sight, and don't make it
difficult at first. You do not want him to get discouraged and give
up. Vary your hiding places and always reward a successful find
with enthusiasm. If you can peek without his seeing you, it's really
rewarding to see him starting to rely on his nose to help locate
you, tracking the most recent trail of scent you have left on the
way to your hiding place.

To make this step more difficult, let somebody take him outside for a walk while you hide, and conceal yourself more this
time. To help him, open a window slightly to create an air current
that will carry your scent toward the open door of the room.
When he's brought back in, tell the person helping you to give him
a command, such as "Find Mary," or "Find John." He will probably first look where you were when he went out. Let him work at
it, encouraged by whomever walked him outside. If it takes too
long, call his name just once to give him the incentive, then have
both of them look for you together. When the find is made, make
a big fuss over his accomplishment. He will grasp the idea fast, and
each time it will be easier, and he will find you more rapidly. With
this new game, you are actually teaching him the basics of Search
and Track. Never scold him for finding you on his own, even if you
don't feel like being found, like when you are taking a nap. He's

just doing what you taught him but is not waiting for the command. Later, you can hide outdoors and have him search for you. Let him see you leave so that he knows you're outside. Outdoor hiding places can be endless and can vary from the easy finds to difficult and challenging finds for your pal. Just train in easy stages and make it fun!

Find the Ball

Another enjoyable game that develops into a good workout for your dog is to throw a ball and have him find it. Dogs usually are interested in balls, especially bright-colored, bouncy ones that are exciting with motion. A good-sized field away from the danger of highway traffic is an excellent place to start this game, provided the space is available for your use. If not, a good substitute is a safely fenced large yard.

Start first with some gentle teasing to get him excited over the ball, then toss it a short distance and ask him to get it. Race toward it yourself. If you get there first, pick it up and show him what you have found, let him smell it, then repeat the motion a couple of times. Soon he will catch on to the new game. If he beats you to the ball but doesn't pick it up, then do it for him. Put it in his mouth and have him hold it for a few moments, praising him to let him know that this is part of the game. Put your retrieving command to use here; make it pay off.

Then take a walk around the field with him and quietly drop the ball somewhere along the way. Turn around and signal in the direction from which you came. Make believe that you are throwing the ball, and send him for it. Watch his reactions closely, especially when he uses his nose as he gets near the ball. Remember how he acts, because this may be of great help when you need to learn to "read" your dog. Give him lots of praise as he brings the ball to you. This game can become quite advanced and involved if you progress gradually to greater degrees of difficulty and give him additional challenges.

Another step in furthering his training is to start teaching him to identify objects by their names. Begin this game in the house and be very patient, because it requires consistent word association by repetition and praise. Use his own toys at first, such as "Get your ball" (bone, strap, chew stick). Don't correct if he brings a wrong article but *does* bring you something! You can branch out until his vocabulary includes your slippers, key case, wallet, eyeglasses case, gloves, and other items. Be sure that your scent is on the object, at least at the beginning, to give him extra help. And never send him on a wild-goose chase in which there is nothing to bring back. Also, don't expect his find to be lightning fast. Give him time.

Get the Paper

Once he has learned to find and bring an article that you have scented, the fun can really start. One chore that you can teach him is to bring in the newspaper, but remember to start by first going out yourself after its arrival and handling it to put your scent on it. Then call him, open the door, and give him the command to bring it to you as you point to it. Always use the same words, such as Get the Paper. Praise him, thank him, then sit down and read the paper. Later, fold it up again and, when he's not looking, take it outside and drop it a short distance from where it was. This will be extra practice to prepare him to *look* for it. We all know that paperboys can aim quite well, but not so accurately that they can land the paper in the same spot every time!

Let your dog use his nose to hunt for it, as long as he knows what it is that you want. Don't send him for it as soon as you return to the house, let the paper lie there for awhile. Praise him so that he knows he's doing what you want. When you're sure that he has the idea, send him for a paper that you haven't handled. No doubt just the odor of the printer's ink, the scent left by the regular newsboy, and the looks of the newspaper associated with the name "paper" will already have clicked in his mind. Get down on your knees and give him the praise he deserves. Tell him how proud you are of him and watch how pleased he'll be with himself. This command can be carried over to magazines, small packages, and other paper items.

Playing "Rescue"

From here, you can progress to a game of hide and seek around the house, starting with a member of the family and combining the Find with the already learned command of Speak. Continue the game to where one of the family can go outside and hide behind a tree or bush, in a shed, or a place where he can be found easily. Have the person sit or lie down and help with the training by telling the dog to Speak when he gets near. Go to the "found" party, help him up, and give your dog praise. "Help" the party into the house. Now your dog has participated in a simulated rescue that might actually happen someday.

When staging this game, wait for fifteen or twenty minutes before sending your dog, then give the command "Find Charlie" or whoever is lost, and go along to help look for him. Keep up the pretense of looking as you repeat the Find command. Try to work downwind of the person so that his scent will be brought toward your dog as he searches. As soon as you hear your dog Speak, let him know by your voice how happy you are, and finish acting out the drama. Don't repeat this often, because he might get the idea that you don't really mean it. But each time, make the find a little more difficult and challenging, but never too hard for him to handle. If this happens, go back to staging easier finds and reward him with great enthusiasm. You know, a situation like this could happen in real life and *your* dog could become a hero! It is rewarding just to watch your dog in such a situation and see how he puts his nose to work.

If you ever decide to earn a Tracking Dog title (provided you own a purebred, registered dog), this little game will actually be a basic foundation to get you started.

You also can get your dog to find a stranger, one who is not a member of the family or a frequent visitor. Set it up first with the person visiting your house and leaving an object behind, such as a glove, a scarf, or anything that has his scent on it. After he has been gone for a few minutes (and be sure that he goes in a predetermined path and direction), "discover" the article left behind and go to the door, making believe that you are calling him to tell him he forgot something. Take your dog and tell him to "Find Frank" or whoever, show him the article, and the two of you go after your friend. Repeat your calling and urge your dog to help you. Be sure to get him to Speak as he finds the person. Your mission will be completed, the article will be returned, and everyone will be happy. Your own imagination can run riot from now on, but don't try to fool your dog and don't invent situations that are too difficult. Keep it fun, even though you're working on something that could be very serious.

Carrying and Bringing the Lead

Your previous teaching of Take, Hold, and Carry can now be the means of getting your dog to be a useful helper as you perform your own regular daily chores. He's your companion now, so take him with you and give him something to do. He'll be proud to do it as long as he thinks that he is helping you.

Take him to your mailbox and to the post office and give him a piece of mail to carry; a rolled up circular or a small magazine or catalog. Don't let him chew or mouth it; teach him to treat it carefully and gently. Give him a small package that he can manage and let him carry it into the house. You can even teach him to carry messages and articles to another person in the house, commanding "Take it to Frank" or whoever. Make sure that the person receiving it uses the right release command and praises the dog properly as a reward.

You can also teach your dog to bring his lead to you when he wants to go outside. Always refer to it by name, and prepare it, at first, by folding it and wrapping it with a rubber band. When he speaks, asking to go out, tell him Get Your Lead, and show him where you've put it so that he can reach it easily. Teach him to pick it up and bring it to you, then reward him with praise *and* by taking him out. When he's done this a few times, fold the lead so that one end is hanging free several inches and the rest is wrapped. Get him used to handling it like this and not tripping and stepping on it (just as he got used to a short cord before you started lead-breaking him). Eventually, he'll be able to carry the lead without its being folded for him. Be consistent and keep it in the same place so that he'll know where it is when he wants to go for a walk. Going for a walk can be much more fun if he begins it this way.

If you like to entertain for hospitals, schools, children's homes, and other groups, a volunteer who can stage a show with a dog is always in demand. Many tricks can be worked up with a little imagination and practice. Your dog can demonstrate that he knows the difference between a ten-dollar and one-dollar bill when you send him out for one of them and *your scent* is on the one you want him to get! Put several wallets on the floor and ask him to pick yours and bring it back. Ask him to find the flag of his country among several in a rack, after you have touched the right one.

Teach him to carry a small basket holding candy, balloons, or gum, and have him distribute the contents to the children. Having him deliver flowers to patients in a convalescent home is another enjoyable activity. You can also teach him to take another dog for a walk. Projects like this can be exceptionally rewarding and so very much appreciated. The limits of your own imagination and the amount of time you can devote will be your only limitations. Have fun with your entertaining—just don't expect your pal to perform impossible or extremely difficult feats. Keep it fun for *him*, too!

Fig. 11-5. Your dog will love to help by fetching the morning paper.

Chapter 12
TRAVELING
WITH YOUR DOG

The title of this chapter makes you think about getting into a car and heading for parts unknown, perhaps for a trip of several thousand miles. But we had better take first things first and teach some of the necessary "little" exercises before we tackle the ultimate goal: having a contented and relaxed companion with you, no matter what your mode of transportation or your destination.

Elevators

For instance, suppose you live in an apartment building or condominium that has an elevator, or that you have a friend you like to visit who lives in one. And suppose your dog has never experienced that sudden going-up or going-down sensation. It can be traumatic and confusing to him. Remember the first time you rode in one and how your stomach felt, especially if the start and stop were sudden? Rather than put your pal through this with no warning or preparation, let's see how we can make it easier for him.

If you have a puppy or a small dog, you can start by holding him in your arms, giving him the physical contact of your body that instills his trust in you. If your dog is larger and you cannot lift him, adapt the instructions as best as you can and make the introduction gradually as you progress through the various steps.

First, pick up your dog and hold him in your arms, making sure that he relaxes by listening to your pleasant and reassuring voice. Repeat this in different environments both inside and outside, standing still and moving. Hold him securely so that there is no danger of dropping him, then suddenly lower your arms to at least waist level to make him feel the dropping sensation. Reassure him and bring him back up again in your arms, laughing as though nothing had happened. During your practice, try the reverse and make a sudden move when raising him back to normal position. Then combine the two and make it into a new fun game, always keeping his confidence and trust in you. If you can keep him relaxed during this practice, then you are ready to try the elevator.

But first comes the introduction. Put the lead on your dog and snap it onto the dead ring if you're using a slip collar. Approach the elevator and see to it that your dog is facing the center of the door. This way he'll get used to any rush of air caused by the elevator moving and to high-frequency sounds that you and I might not even detect but that could be very disturbing to his ears. Watch for his reactions and reassure him if you see his ears lay back, his tail go down, his expression become confused, or his body tremble. Let him watch the door open and close. Don't try to enter the elevator yet—just watch. Then praise him and heel him away from it a short distance.

Return to your position in front of the door and call the elevator to your floor again. As the door opens, reach in immediately to press the "door hold" button or emergency hold switch so that the door will not close on your dog as you move inside with him. Practice this exercise when the elevator is being used minimally to make it easier for both of you. It only adds to your problems if there are other passengers on your first ride. Later it will not matter, because your dog will have become accustomed to the sensation of going up and down, the noise, the smells, and other distractions.

Take a position away from, but facing, the door and within reach of the control panel. Release the car and press the "down" button. Watch your dog carefully, and if you see signs of fear or his getting upset, press the "stop" button. Reassure him that all is well and try again. When you've managed two or three floors by stops in between, leave the elevator carefully, and walk away slowly so that he hears the closing door behind him. Now give lots of praise.

Use the same caution on approaching the elevator as you return, keeping your dog in correct position and being careful of the door as you enter. As you start up, having pressed the button, keep your dog's attention on you by talking to him. When the car stops for you to get off, control him properly so that he leaves *with you*. Don't allow him to bolt for the opening.

When you're riding with other people who are getting on or off at different floors other than the one you want, be sure that your dog is under control and is not trying to move because he sees other people moving. Also reassure the other occupants that your dog is friendly and trained and is your companion. We do occasionally meet people who are afraid of dogs and don't trust them (even though it is difficult for us to understand WHY), so we should allay their fears to the best of our ability.

Don't rush this training; proceed at a pace suited to your own dog. Some dogs adapt to the new situation much more rapidly than others, so let him tell you how fast to go. Maybe he'll take to it so well that he will make you think he's been riding elevators all his life! Don't be afraid to speak up and spread the good word on how a little training of your canine companion can open up the doors of the world to you (and not just elevator doors!) to make your life so much more enjoyable.

Car Safety

We've already covered some of the basic advice on getting your dog used to a car and the cautionary steps to try to avoid car sickness when we first talked about bringing a puppy home. Seeing motion outside the car, as well as sounds and vibrations, are usually the contributing factors to car sickness, so training must be done in short and easy doses.

There are some additional cautionary points we would like to bring to your attention, one of the most important dealing with your pet's safety concerning open windows. If you allow your dog to travel, as many thoughtless people do, with his head out the window, you're inviting trouble. It is downright dangerous! An unexpected, sudden braking stop can catapult him right through the window. It is also possible that a bug or foreign object will be blown into an eye or an ear, also with serious results. And a dog riding like this is usually a distraction and worry, affecting the safety of the driver, the passengers, and other people who might be involved if it causes an accident.

This doesn't mean that the windows have to be kept closed tightly, because some air should be circulating to prevent any accumulation of deadly carbon monoxide exhaust fumes (deadly to people as well as to dogs).

Another very real and proven danger is leaving your pet in your parked car in the sun, even with all the windows down a little. The temperature *inside* the car can rise so drastically and fast that in just *ten* minutes it can reach the point of causing a heat stroke, resulting in a tragic fatality. If you doubt this, hang a thermometer inside your car, park it in the sun (*without* your dog!), even if the outside temperature is no more than 80, then return in fifteen or twenty minutes and see what it reads! And a reading of 106 can cause heat prostration in your pal. Think about it. Plan ahead, and if you have to leave your car parked in the sun or with the motor running (bad practice anyway) and he would be alone, please leave him home.

As we travel around the country, we're amazed to see how many people drive pickup trucks and have their dog riding in the open truck behind the cab. What are they thinking of? No matter how well-trained the dog might be, some distraction might trigger him to jump out, such as a strange dog chasing the truck, a cat, or squirrel, or other wild animal moving near or on the road, or an unexpected collision. In addition to this, the dog is subjected to all

Fig. 12-1. **It is dangerous to allow a dog to travel this way.**

Fig. 12-2. **Window down a bit for air, but still providing protection.**

the weather elements and to the bumps and sudden swerves throwing him around in the back. Try taking his place in the back of a pickup, and don't use your hands to hold on. He doesn't have any, does he?

If it's absolutely necessary for your dog to ride back there, at least give him some safety and protection. The following picture will help you construct a safety device to which he can be fastened without completely confining him. In addition to this, construct some kind of shield above his area so that he will be protected from the burning sun or a bad storm. Be sure to fasten into the dead or nonworking ring if he's wearing a slip collar, or better yet, use a regular flat collar to make sure that he is comfortable and in no danger. If he has no protection, he can so easily be injured severely or even killed upon a sudden braking stop or an unavoidable collision.

All you need to do is install a storm door chain assembly that includes a compression spring at each of the two outside corners behind the cab. You can shorten or lengthen the chain if necessary, depending mainly on the width of the pickup, allowing room for the dog to lie down.

The reason for using the chain in this assembly is to avoid the dog's being able to chew his way free and jump out, perhaps into heavy traffic. Put your dog's comfort and safety *first,* and he'll repay you many times over. Remember, *you* are responsible for him, *not* vice versa!

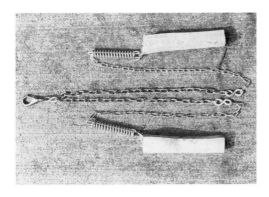

Fig. 12-3. Spring coil with chain and collar attached. May be installed in two front corners of pickup box, or on the floor of vans or wagons.

Vans and Station Wagons

The increasingly popular vans and the ever dependable station wagons offer more leeway for vacation trips that not only can include the whole family, the luggage, and camping and sporting equipment, but the family pets as well. Here you definitely need a secured wire crate, ample in size for your dog to stand up and lie down in comfort and fixed so that it cannot slide or tip over when

Fig. 12-4.   A dog secured in this way can ride safely in the back of a pickup truck.

put in place. Make it easily accessible and don't pile articles close to it so that his view is obstructed or his air is limited. Be sure to take along his water and food dishes, as well as his regular food and a supply of cool water from home. A change of water can upset his digestive system quickly. By starting with your own water supply, you can gradually mix other water with it as you travel, thus greatly reducing the possible effects of a sudden complete change.

Swimming and Boating

If you enjoy swimming and boating and your dog is going to be a real companion, you will also want his company there. But first, does he know how to swim? Some dogs fear the water and have to be taught. And naturally, if you go out in any type of boat, he first must know how to swim before being introduced to a boat.

Swimming—Even though you may believe that any dog will swim and all you need to do is throw him in, this is the quickest way to give him such a traumatic experience that he'll avoid going into

Fig. 12-5. Crates provide safety for van passengers.

water for the rest of his life. Such an act could destroy all the confidence that has been built between the two of you thus far. We once saw a retriever get panicky in the water and start flailing and creating his own little whirlpool, pulling himself down into it. If help had not been immediately available, he most certainly would have met his end. Teaching your dog to swim and being sure that he can handle himself in the water, no matter how deep, is the only way to avoid such a terrible experience.

To start, first find a beach or a shallow shoreline of a lake or pond, one that is not off limits to dogs and one that is not crowded. Be sure to dress for the occasion, because you're going to get wet! Don't expect your *dog* to get wet if you are unwilling to share the water with him!

With your dog on lead, using the dead ring of the collar, start walking along the shore, positioning yourself between him and the water. This way, as you move closer, you'll be the first to step into the water. When he sees that you are not afraid and that it doesn't harm you, it builds his confidence and removes any fear he may have. Laugh and talk to him as you move. Praise him, but don't give in to him and pick him up. If he should panic and try to pull away, just come out of the water and begin again. Maybe you went too fast the first time; try going slower and make it more fun.

When you see that he doesn't mind his feet being wet, move out farther, but go slowly and carefully. Moving into deeper water too fast may upset the applecart and undo all you have accomplished. This is why the shallow shoreline is important. Watch your dog carefully and learn to read him by his actions. You'll be able to tell if you are going too fast and if he is enjoying the new experience.

If he's having fun romping in the shallow water with you, start running a bit so that the water splashes on him. Laugh and have fun as you go short distances, getting him wet, gradually getting in deep enough that his tummy is in the water. Don't keep him in if he begins to show fear or resentment. Even if he does not, it's time to go out and sit on the beach for a little rest. If all is well, then call him and run into the water *with* him, *not* ahead of him, and only out to the same depth in which you already have been.

For the next step, be prepared to get really wet! Walk into the water with your pal, talking as you go, but do not use his name.

You don't want his attention on you right now. Let him concentrate on the new project at hand. As you go into deeper water, watch him, and when he starts to hold his head higher, remove the lead and put it away. Then, as you reassure him with your tone of voice, place your hand lightly under his chin and use your other hand as a balance guide to keep his body level. Be sure that his feet are not touching bottom, and move slowly at that depth, parallel to the shore. As he starts propelling himself forward to keep abreast of you, start to release the hand under his chin and let him take over on his own. Let him feel a slight pressure of your other hand under his body to reassure him of your presence if he needs help.

As you see him gaining self-confidence in the water, remove your hands completely, first the one under his chin, then the other one. Keep moving, but gently turn toward the shore. When he starts to walk on the bottom, put the lead back on his collar, just to play safe. Don't take a chance on his running toward a highway or group of people. Give him lots of praise for his accomplishment. From this point, you can gradually increase your excursions together in the water, both in distance and length of time. Just don't overdo it and allow him to get exhausted. Keep it fun all the way.

Boating—Now you can teach your companion proper behavior for riding in a boat. As with any situation that is new to him, the introduction comes first. You will follow methods similar to those used in preparing your dog to ride in a car. No matter what kind of boat—a canoe, rowboat, sailboat, or motorboat—these steps are very important.

Let us begin with the canoe or rowboat, because both are completely open, and the urge to jump out can be inviting, especially when motion is created with the paddles or oars as they disturb the water. This attraction might lead to trouble that can be prevented with proper training.

For his first introduction, *lift* him into the boat; *don't* make him jump into it. Enter the boat yourself at the same time and be sure that he is under control with the lead fastened to the dead ring if he's wearing a slip collar. Use a plain buckled collar if you prefer, fastened so that it will not slip over his head. Hold the lead as close to the collar as necessary to keep him near you so that you can reassure him and prevent him from trying to jump. Let the boat drift at first to get your dog used to the rolling motion caused by the water. Watch him for any reaction, remembering that some dogs do get seasick as well as car sick, just as humans do. Be ready to get him to shore immediately if necessary, and don't scold him.

If all is going well, have a friend or other family member paddle or row slowly and easily as you talk to your dog and keep his attention on you. Pet him and reassure him that all is as it should be. Soon you'll see that he is relaxing and beginning to enjoy his outing on the water with you. Repeat this a few times until you are sure of his reactions and your control over him. Use your obedience commands of Sit, Stay, and Down-Stay and when you return to shore, give him a Wait command, then lift him out. Don't allow him to jump out. You can later teach him to enter and leave the boat on your command, and *only* on command. This will prevent any "unauthorized" jumping from the boat. If you hunt ducks and have a special type of boat, you may have to adjust your training for this due to the limited space for your dog. He may have to jump out before you when leaving and enter after you are settled in your seat. Show and teach your dog to enjoy your boat as much as you do, and have fun together.

Now let's consider the variations that apply to sailboats. First, you must consider the moving boom. A second condition is the sound of the sails being hoisted and the wind in the sails once you're underway. If you have an auxiliary motor, your dog should become familiar with that sound. All of the introductions to the new conditions and the obedience training should be the responsibility of one person whose help is not needed for crewing the sailboat.

Much of this work can be done right at the dock before the boat is moving under sail. The person should be one whom your dog knows and trusts, one in whose presence he can be completely relaxed and who is willing to progress slowly. If this person is someone other than yourself, be sure that he will use a good tone of voice and give bodily contact when necessary. Just be content to take it slow and easy. After all, you do want your pal to learn to travel with you and enjoy the activities you do, so be cautious about how this new environment is presented to him. Don't risk doing anything that will cause fear, resentment, or mistrust of you.

Now let us consider powerboats. The first difference here, naturally, is the vibration of the motor in addition to the sound. Because dogs are very aware of this vibration through sensation in their feet, it can cause concern and apprehension in their minds. They do need reassurance, and, regardless of the size of the boat, they should be kept on lead for their own protection.

Keeping him on lead until you are sure of his conduct and his ability to gain his "sea legs" and keep his balance can prevent an accident that might otherwise occur. The spray of water at the stern from the wake created by the motor is often very attractive, and many dogs like to try to grab it. A fall overboard could mark the fatal end of your pal, because the props of a motor are nothing to tangle with! And a sudden bump or lurch to one side could cause a bad injury if your dog is unaccustomed to responding with quick reflexes. Show the same concern for him that you would for a young, innocent child.

Keeping Him in the Trunk?

Now, on to another means of transporting dogs that exists all too frequently (in our opinion). Nevertheless, this does occur, and we must face it and offer ways in which to improve the situation. This is the practice of some hunters, farmers, and ranchers of carrying their dogs in the trunk of a car. Why? Just because they don't trust them inside the car? Maybe they will get it dirty or leave some dog hair on the cushions?

Usually all that people do is tie the trunk down enough to leave a small air space. The prevalence of exhaust gases in the trunk area make it practically a death chamber. At best, the gases will most likely affect a dog's most prized faculty—his noseability for hunting and for other work chores, as well as his own happiness in daily living. Constant exposure to these killing fumes can deaden or kill the nerve endings on the sensors in the membranes of the nasal cavity and impair the dog's ability to smell. It's hard for us to imagine just how keen this is in a normal dog, since some researchers have estimated that it is one million times greater than that of a human!

We all know that the trunk of a car is not insulated or lined. Even road dirt can creep in, as well as fumes. The rays of the sun also beat down on it, making it much hotter.

Commercially made trunk ventilators (advertised in hunting magazines) are available, and they can improve the situation to some extent. A better idea is to get a small trailer to tow behind your car, provided it is built so that exhaust fumes from the car are avoided and it gets ample fresh air.

Whatever you do, look at it from the dog's point of view and imagine how *you* would react if you changed places with *him*. If you follow this policy all through your life with him, you'll both be happy and enjoy each other.

Fig. 12-6. This dog has been taken beyond swimming in training and has learned to tow a boat (water rescue).

Chapter 13
ADVANCING
IN TRAINING

In this chapter, our instructions will be directed specifically to those people who have no particular handicap and do not need special aids to assist their moving. First, we'll review the heeling in general, although most of this has already been covered for those in wheelchairs or those using walkers or crutches.

First to consider is the importance of breaking each exercise into small but important steps. Each step may be likened to another block in the firm, reliable foundation that you are building. And you must be familiar with the progression of these steps so that your timing won't suffer from your having to stop and think about what comes next.

Another point that merits re-emphasizing is the fact that the slip ring of a training collar is used only for corrections or for gaining control of a dog. Remember that a correction is *not* made when your dog does not yet know the right way to perform an exercise. He must first be shown, then the exercise must be repeated and associated with a command and/or signal to establish a pattern. Only he can let you know if he has truly learned it. After you have reached this point with him and are absolutely sure that he knows, then a correction might be in order if you know he's deliberately disobeying you. But don't dwell on it—make it effective and quick, then put him to work immediately to take his mind off it. Don't stand there and scold him, because it will do neither of you any good. If you are getting good results with a plain buckled collar, all the better. Continue with it, for it's much more comfortable for your pal. And never use your feet or your knees to correct your dog, because you want him to completely trust you and want to be close to you.

To review our recommendation for handling the lead, use both hands and keep them no higher than the level of your waist. Start by putting the loop over the thumb of your hand (if your dog is to your left, use your right hand; if he is to your right, use your left hand), then fold the lead into that hand, leaving only enough to reach your dog's collar without having to pull on it when he's at Heel position. You can release the lead anytime you wish by opening your hand, but you'll still have the lead over your thumb. Use the other hand on the lead and near the collar in such a manner that you can control its position just by sliding it wherever needed as you work, guiding your dog closer to you if he is lagging or forging or is too wide in his heeling, or farther from you if he is crowding. Remember to use your pleasant tone of voice to keep his attention. Carry on a conversation with him and make it fun.

As we go into the Heeling practice in more detail, we will combine the already learned exercises of Stand, Sit, and Down along with the moving and explain the importance of your footwork in cueing your dog.

Remember that when we say "Heel position," here it means that your dog is either at your left or your right side (you have made the choice for a particular reason), and his shoulder is about even with your knee—close to you but not touching so that he will not interfere with your own movement. (Note that AKC obedience regulations require that all dogs *must* heel on the left side.)

As you start moving in your practice sessions, first use your dog's name for attention, then give the command Heel as you step out on the foot nearest your dog. This will become his guide and will cue him as to whether or not he's expected to move with you. Make your halts smooth; don't "jump into them" as you might expect a serviceman to do in drilling under a tough sergeant. Again, pay attention to your footwork, and make your last foot in motion the one next to your dog. Be consistent in this, and you'll find your dog being consistent with straight sits. Also, check yourself on the halts, and be sure that you're not pulling the lead across your body and making your dog sit at an angle. If you need to use your lead to remind him of the Sit, make the motion upward and straight back with your guide hand, accompanied by the command if necessary.

Fig. 13-1. Practicing the recall off lead.

When making turns while practicing the Heel, first get used to them without your dog. Imagine where he will be and think about your feet. Your main concern should be to keep them out of his way as much as possible, giving him a clear track if you want to avoid his lagging or developing a fear of your feet. It's easy to remember the footwork for the turns, because you pivot on the toe of your left foot and step out with the right on the *left* turn, and pivot on the toe of your right foot and step out with the left on the *right* turn. On the about turn, avoid the military style, because it leaves one foot in back as you turn and forces your dog to lag and wait for you while you get it out of his way. Just keep your feet as close together as possible when you turn, and lead out immediately, even if you only make half a step as you move forward. Be consistent with your footwork, and your dog will learn that he can depend on your feet to give him cues about your intended direction of movement.

Another interesting exercise that also helps to teach your dog what Heel means and aids a dog that heels around behind on the "finish from in front" is the "left about turn" for the heelers on the left side. (This would be a "right about turn" for those heeling on the right side.) As you move forward (and with your lead gathered in the hand away from your dog), turn toward your dog and, at the same time, guide him around behind you, transferring your lead to the other hand behind you. As you complete your about turn and step out, your dog will have completed his turn behind you and will be in correct heeling position. At first this may seem a bit confusing, but it becomes fun and affords some interesting variety in your patterns.

As you teach any of the turns, remember to speak your dog's name to be sure that you have his attention as you start the turn. Then praise him with that magic word "G-o-o-o-o-d!" This will assure him that he's doing his lesson right and will eliminate any need for yanking him into position, which should be avoided. Your goal in teaching your dog to heel properly is to keep each other out of the other one's way, thus avoiding accidents.

Now let's get into some practice sessions, and we will give you a few ideas to help you make them interesting. These will help keep your dog sharp and should apply to both heeling on lead and off lead. A word of caution—your dog is not ready to work off lead if you still need to guide him with it and use extra commands or signals. He should be completely reliable in carrying out your commands. Each command should be given only one time, and your dog should work on a completely loose lead before you try him without the lead.

Familiarize yourself with the routines before you start to work with your dog. Get them set in your mind, and you might go through them first without him, making sure that you understand what you're going to do.

As you move forward, increase your pace just enough to bring a smooth, rhythmic motion into your dog's gait. Go no more than ten or twelve feet before changing, such as right turn, slow, normal, left turn, about turn, complete circle to the left, left about, fast, normal, complete circle to the right. Bring a halt into the pattern frequently, and don't repeat the exercises twice in the same sequence. Learn to change them around so that your dog will not develop a habit of doing exercises in a given pattern. Keep your dog's attention, and learn to read him if you find that you are losing that attention. It may be that your practice is too long and he's tired. Or perhaps he needs to be picked up with your tone of voice. Maybe just a short quick step away from him, when he least expects it, will jog his thoughts back to where they should be.

To refresh your memory on doing the circles to the left and the right while heeling, refer to the instruction given in Chapter 7. This is an excellent way to teach your dog to stay in the proper position, regardless of whether you're praticing for show competition or are simply weaving through pedestrian traffic. Put the circles together to practice a Figure-8 exercise, using two inanimate objects to walk around about eight to ten feet apart. They can be chairs, posts, boxes, or whatever is handy and convenient for you. It's not wise to use other dogs on a Sit-Stay, because somebody's tail might get stepped on (or run over if a wheelchair is involved).

When practicing the Figure-8, it's advisable to make your first circle toward your dog (circle left if he heels on the left, circle right if he heels on the right). Leave enough space between you and the "post" so that your dog doesn't get crowded and is forced to lag. Keep this same space all the way around the "post," then cross over on a straight line and make the other circle, turning evenly again and not bumping the "post." This time, your dog will be on the outside of the circle because you are going in the opposite direction. Try to keep your same speed doing both circles, and let your dog do his own adjusting as he goes from making a smaller circle to a larger one. Also, practice your halts in the turns, as well as on the straight cross-overs.

Review Chapter 7 for instructions in teaching the Stay and Wait commands, and understand the difference between them. Also, work on the Recall exercise, teaching your dog to Come on command.

To complete this exercise, you must also teach your dog to go to the Heel position after he has come to you. And here we remind you that if you plan to train for show competition, your dog must sit in front of you when you call him and must heel at your left side. This also means that he will have to come into Heel position on command from the Sit position in front of you. If you prefer, for personal reasons, that he not sit in front but continue immediately to Heel position, then you can eliminate that part of the exercise.

Now we come to the question, which direction shall he go to Heel—toward the side of his normal heeling, or around and behind you, then into the Sit? To find the answer, we let the dog tell us, because he often shows a definite preference. We're not sure if dogs are left-handed and right-handed as people are, but our experience over the years definitely points to that conclusion. Try your dog both ways, and if you see him balking, holding back, or putting on his brakes in one direction and not in the other, then he is trying to tell you something. He likes one way better than the other, so why argue with him? Go the easy way!

Your commands as you begin to teach the exercise should be his name (for attention), Come (to get him moving), Heel (or whatever your choice is for the exercise), and Sit (to let him know what you expect of him when he gets into position). Remember to use your lead to *guide* him as he is moving and your voice to encourage him. If he's finishing around behind you, try to make a smooth transfer of your folded lead from one hand to the other as he moves in back of you, then guide him into the Sit. If finishing to the side, guide him in a circle pattern *away* from you, making the circle large enough to allow him to turn *toward* you, but behind, as he completes the circle and comes into the Sit at the right spot. As he gets used to the pattern, start to ease off on the guiding and work with a loose lead. Then eliminate the extra commands, keeping just the one word for the exercise. In addition to the more frequently used command of Heel, we have heard By Me, Swing, and others.

For best results in teaching your dog to Finish directly from the recall without the Sit in front, start practicing it when he's coming toward you. Make your recalls short distances, and remember to give the commands to Heel and then to Sit, timing them with his action. If you are not yet sure of the recalls, go back to Chapter 7 for some refresher work and make sure that your dog is responding well to the Come before you add the new exercise. Remember to depend upon your voice for control as you work, rather than your lead, because the lead is only for guiding. Don't jerk it, just keep it slightly snug and in the direction of travel until he knows what you want him to do. Then work on a loose lead.

When your dog is working reliably on a loose lead, doing both the Recall and the Finish, and the recall distance has been gradually increased to twenty or thirty feet, you can begin to think about practicing the exercise *off* lead. However, you must understand that to get satisfactory results, you must return to basics and start from a short distance, leaving your dog no more than a lead's length away from you. Vary your practice so that he won't get into a habit of anticipating what comes next and doing it before you command him. When he sits in front, part of the time you do the moving, circling him back to Heel position. And part of the time, give him the command to Finish to have him come into Heel position by you. As he improves in his performance, you can gradually increase the distance. If you find any lack of attention or diminishing of a prompt response developing, do not hesitate to backtrack in your training. Shorten and vary the distance, and think about at what point you probably went too fast. Learn to analyze yourself to determine what is causing your dog's behavior.

Signals

So far in your training, except for the commands of Wait and Stay, you've been teaching and practicing only the voice commands for the different exercises. Now we are going to help you

Fig. 13-2. Teaching the Finish to left.

Fig. 13-3. Teaching the Finish to right.

round out his education so your dog will be an even more valuable companion by teaching him to respond to hand signals and whistles.

A signal can often be more effective than your voice as long as your dog's attention is focused on you and your actions. Many exercises in obedience are also performed on signals, even in competition, and one level requires the dog to respond entirely to hand signals. Others are part signal, part command, and any of them may be executed by choice with signals. In field trial retrieving, it is a definite necessity for dogs to respond to direction signals at a goodly distance from their handlers. And signals of different whistle patterns are an integral part of the performance of dogs that herd sheep. It's a thrilling sight to watch beautifully trained dogs doing what is expected of them in a Utility Obedience class at a show, in Retriever Field Trials, and at Sheep Herding Trials.

The main points to remember about the hand signals are that they should be given so that your dog can see them from start to finish from *his* eye level; your clothing should be color-contrasted as viewed by him against the background; signals should not be given as a flash; and they are taught in the beginning by association with the voice command and by doing them on lead.

You should first practice signals in front of a mirror before you work with your dog, always imagining how they will look to him. Our years of experience have borne out the success and effectiveness of the signals given as we describe them.

To give the signal to Heel forward, use the hand nearest the dog and start the motion from outside his body and a bit forward of his head (so that he can see it). Sweep your hand across in front of him and end the movement in front of yourself, about waist high. Then return your hand to normal position at your side.

The Stay signal begins in front of you and sweeps across, stopping when the palm of your hand is in line with the front of your dog's head, so that he can look diretly at it. It's not necessary to bend down for a small dog and get it at his eye level, for he will see it if you have dog attention. Then return your hand to normal position. (Fig. 6-6).

The Wait signal is the same except for the fact that it *continues past* the head instead of stopping directly in front. Then return to normal position. (Fig. 6-7).

The Come signal is a swinging out from your body of your arm at shoulder height, then bringing it across to the front of your body before returning it to normal. Be sure that the entire motion can be seen by your dog.

The Down signal starts at your side. Raise your arm so that the elbow is no more than shoulder high. Your hand should be up, elbow bent, and palm toward your dog. The movement should reach this point with a sudden stop, hesitate a moment, then return to normal.

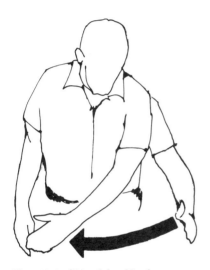

Fig. 13-4. Signal for Heel.

Fig. 13-5. Signal for Come.

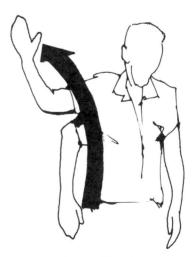

Fig. 13-6. Down Signal.

There are several variations of the Stand signal. Sometimes one will be more effective than another, depending on the reaction of the individual dog or how comfortable the handler will be. We prefer a signal that starts with the arm across the body waist high and swings out parallel to the floor, palm facing down, ending out in front of the dog's head. Return it to normal position when your dog remains in position. Remember that you must come to a halt at the same time, too, when you are practicing this in motion.

The Finish to Heel signal is done with the hand and arm on the side toward which the dog moves, whether to the left or to the right. This is just a swinging circular sweep to the left or right, then returning to normal. Be careful that you don't unconsciously develop a turning of your head or body with the signal, because it is entirely unnecessary and can throw your dog off from coming into the correct Heel position.

The signal to Go Out is usually used in conjunction with the verbal command, rather than in place of it. However, it is sometimes used alone, especially in field trials. The hand nearest the dog is lined up with the intended direction of travel, about waist high, then thrust forward past the dog's head as the command Go! is given.

Fig. 13-7. Finish to left.

Fig. 13-8. Finish to right.

In teaching your dog to "Take A Line," that is, to go in a definite direction for a specific reason, the placing of your hand is very important. Bend your body slightly to get near enough to your dog so that you can place the back of your hand alongside his face, even with his eyes, pointing in the direction in which you want him to go. Be sure that your thumb is down and out of the way in case he might turn his head suddenly (you don't want to run the risk of poking him in the eye), then give an upward and forward flip of your hand, accompanied by your verbal command to send him on his way. As he leaves, return your hand to normal.

In teaching your dog to go to the left or to the right (used in the Directed Jump in Obedience and also in Field Trials), use your left arm if you want him to go to your left, and use your right arm if you want him to go to your right. Raise it smoothly at your side and extend it full length with no bend in the elbow, palm toward your dog, and stop at shoulder height. Return it to normal as soon as your dog has received the message and starts to respond to it.

A further note can be added about the Go Out signal, as is usually seen in Field Trials. Many handlers embellish this signal somewhat by swinging their arm up as high as possible, then adding some forward flipping of the hand as though they are waving at someone, telling the dogs to Get Back! This is to increase the dogs' distance as they work out in the field away from their handlers.

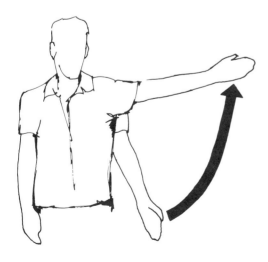

Fig. 13-9. Signal to Go to Left.

Fig. 13-10. Handler signaling dog to Take a Line.

Whistles

Now we come to another topic in advance training—using a whistle for signals. A dog's ears are much more sensitive than those of a person, especially to high-pitched, shrill tones such as whistles and sirens. Thus, a dog will respond very quickly to a whistle and for a much greater distance, because the sound carries farther than our voices. So the whistle can become a very practical piece of equipment in your day-to-day life with your four-footed companion, provided you do a little thinking and be logical about it. You can stop your dog in motion, get his attention so that he will take a signal from you, call him in to you, get him to sit, and numerous other activities. Since you'll probably be using a whistle outdoors, it would be well to bear in mind that cold weather may influence your choice. Steer away from the metal, police-type whistle, because it is uncomfortable against your lips in freezing temperatures. Use a plastic whistle, such as a small or large Acme Thunderer, a Roy Gonya, or a special long-distance style as advertised in sporting magazines.

A "silent whistle" that is adjustable is also available. You can tune it up to such a high frequency that a person cannot hear it, but a dog can. This often is used with dogs that are trained for the movies so that the dogs respond to certain signal commands that are not detected by the average viewer. This type is not good for outdoor work in cold weather, however, because it is made of metal. When you're watching a film or a commercial in which dogs are performing, just for the fun of it, notice where the dog's attention is focused and you will realize that he's getting signals from someone behind the line of cameras.

Fig. 13-11. Plastic Acme Whistles.

When you start to train with a whistle, you have one particular obstacle to overcome. You should learn to hold it to one side of your mouth, and at the same time be able to talk and give commands out of the other side! It can be done with practice, and it leaves your hands free to work with your dog. That's one reason why we prefer a smaller whistle. Before beginning your training, practice blowing the whistle so that you can control the various sounds you want to make. Your dog will learn to respond to each one differently.

The two types of sound for you to master first are a short, sharp blast (this one is easy) and a lower tone trebling, as though you are coaxing with it. When your dog is away from you (a *short* distance and on lead at the beginning), the short blast means that your dog should turn to you for attention, assume a Sit or Down position, and wait for you to give him further direction or command. As you blow the whistle, be ready to immediately give whatever command you wish him to carry out. Be sure that your dog responds and does what you wish him to do on lead, with no extra commands from you, before you start working off lead. Then you may gradually increase your distance.

When you have mastered the treble on the whistle, start teaching this the same way, first at the end of your lead, giving the command Come with it and showing him what you want him to do. Once he has the idea and is responding to both signals, practice them with your regular heeling, substituting the whistle for the commands part of the time. Put variety into the work and don't overdo it or get "whistle-happy." Be very cautious about progressing into the off lead practice, and don't expect miracles all at once. Be content with increasing the distance gradually. *Remember that a mistake cannot be corrected if you're not within controlling distance,* and you'll have to start all over again. You will find, however, that distance control with the whistle can be very rewarding and can save you much footwork.

Staying in His Yard

Our next exercise is one that can prove very difficult to accomplish but is invaluable if you have a home with a front and/or backyard that is not fenced. Naturally, it is best to have the fencing, but sometimes it's not possible. The goal is to teach your dog the boundary lines of the yard(s) and have him realize that he is to respect them. He must learn that he has freedom within that particular area, but is absolutely NOT allowed outside unless he is accompanying you, and is on lead. This project will take time and patience.

To begin, you must devise something visible that your dog can associate with the boundary. You might use a white- or yellow-powdered chalk line, a ribbon of plastic pegged down at necessary points, or even a narrow streak of plain flour. Don't use anything that might be harmful to your dog (such as lime).

Your pal already has learned the recall, both on and off lead, so you have a head start. Later you'll need a lightweight cord long enough to reach from near the door to the closest point of the boundary; also, you will need the tie-out stake that you used when

Fig. 13-12. Make sure that crutches are out of the way when giving the Stay signal to a small dog.

you were breaking him to exercise in a certain area of the back-yard. However, your first lesson will be on the regular training lead and will be like an "introduction." Heel your dog along the visible border. Be ready to immediately make a correction with your lead and voice if he should cross this border, coming in with praise and pleasantness as he returns to the *free* side of the boundary. You should have no trouble keeping him on the proper side just by his responding to his name and praise. The lead should be only a reminder that a correction could come if necessary.

You'll soon find that these reminders are needed less and less. When you observe this, repeat the same lesson with the lead off, but keep it handy so that you can put it back on immediately if necessary. Practice this until you see that, without using your commands, his walks are going according to plan and he appears to understand why the boundary lines are there.

Now get out your long, light line and fasten it to the dead ring of the collar. Use only part of the length at first, but don't get yourself tangled up in the part you are not using! The purpose of the length is to encourage your pal to feel some freedom and have confidence when he's farther than six feet away from you, yet keep control of him in case he needs a reminder. Teach him that he has freedom to roam and play as long as he stays within the designated area and responds to your Come command. Increase the length of the line gradually, depending upon his progress.

Your next step is to put the tie-out stake in position near your entrance door and attach the long line to it, making sure that it is not so long that your dog can cross the boundary line when fastened to it. Attach the line to his collar and go into the house and relax, but check on him through a window. Even if he goes to the boundary, he is still retained safely with the line. If you see him go near the limit and turn back in away from it, let him know what a good dog he is by praising with your voice. You may want to use a special command to cue him that he can play and enjoy his freedom on the long line. You might use the words OK, Go Play, or Have a Good Time, but keep the command consistent so that he knows what you mean. If he tries to go over your boundary line, open the door, and call his name. He'll know what you mean right away, especially when he sees you looking at him. Always praise him for doing the right thing.

If both your front and backyards are without fencing, it will mean a double dose of training, because the same procedure will have to be followed for both.

The next step is a tough one! Here you're going to have to set up a facsimile situation to prepare to counter what might actually happen. You'll need the cooperation of a person that your dog does not know.

Lengthen the light line slightly so that your dog can step over the boundary if he tries. He just might, for your accomplice will be trying to coax him over the line. Be ready, and as the line tightens and rises, step out the door, call your dog's name, and give a *sharp* snap correction with the long line. This should not be severe enough to make him fear you, but effective enough for him to realize that he has made a mistake. This should not be repeated often enough to become routine—just once in awhile as a refresher.

The next step is a big one, because you will find out how effective your training has been so far. It will be *off* lead! And just as in all the other exercises you've taught so far, you go right back to the beginning and work through each step faithfully before proceeding with the next one. That's the only way you're going to reach your goal.

While practicing off lead in the yard, leave the long line stretched out but attached to the tie-out stake. It's not only handy in case you have to revert to its use, it is also a visual reminder to your pal that if he violates the rules, he will have to suffer the consequences.

When you have progressed to the point that you think you can trust him while you go into the house, leave the door slightly ajar so that he cannot hear it opening before he hears his name called. These little rascals are smart, and you have to be devious to fool them.

Don't ever think that your training has been so successful that your dog is dependable enough to resist all kinds of tempta-tions (there ain't no such critter!), and do not leave him out for long periods, no matter how much you trust him. And when you take him with you, put him on lead and go via the sidewalk or a path where there is no boundary line. Don't give him a chance to break the laws, and don't teach him how to break them!

Street Control

Much of your training in street control will be more like enforcing what your dog has learned. However, it will be under many different situations other than what you encounter in your home and own yard.

If you should be doing any of this training in a wheelchair or using a walker, be sure that your equipment is complete with the flag attachment in place. This is for the safety of both you and your dog. When you and your dog are moving along a sidewalk, a path, or a roadway, or are crossing a street, always be alert to prevent any disturbance that might lessen or kill your dog's trust in you and your actions.

At first, choose a place to practice that is not overly crowded. Avoid shopping centers and busy intersections at the start. One of the first problems you will encounter is that of sniffing. This is a dog's way of reading the route to find out who's been this way lately and what may have been left by a human's carelessness in the litter left by the wayside. Sniffing must be controlled and corrected with the lead and voice (or in the case of the lead being attached to the training aid, that and the voice are the correctors).

Teach your dog to pay little attention to strangers by making sure there's no extra slack in the lead. Call his name and talk to keep his attention until this person has passed, then give your dog praise. We do have to acknowledge the fact that some people (fortunately a minority) don't like dogs and respect people who train their dogs to keep their place.

If you meet someone who would like to stop and pass the time of day with you, or even pet your pal and talk to him, that's just fine. Simply halt and tell your dog to Sit, Stay, and don't let him jump on the person. A point like this could be added to the famous text *How to Win Friends and Influence People*.

You might even have to confront someone walking their dog off leash. In that case, just move to the side of the walk, face toward their approach, command Sit, Stay to your dog, and keep control of him. Answer if you're spoken to, but if your dog growls or barks, give him a sharp slap correction under his chin. Keep him under control and praise him. Should the strange dog be too bold and curious and come too close, especially if he is alone, use your harshest tone of voice to chase him away. Threaten him so that he'll head for parts unknown, keeping your own dog in the Sit. Never take off to try to chase him away, because this will only motivate your dog to do the same thing.

When you've mastered these somewhat simple situations, look for more of a challenge, such as heeling near the entrance to a popular department store or supermarket with people going in all directions. Don't barge into the middle of all this unless you want your dog to come home with a nervous breakdown! Begin by taking up a position nearby where the bustle can be observed but where you won't be a part of it. Lean up against the building, out of the way, and have your dog sit by you as you both watch and listen. Watch his reaction, and you'll be able to tell when he's getting used to it and is relaxing. To let him know that most strangers are friendly, pick out one and strike up a short conversation. This may even lead to a conversation about your dog, his breed, or his training, and at the same time will build up a good impression of friendly strangers in your dog's mind.

You may have to adjust the order of these training sessions to your own needs, but this is up to you. For example, we'll now take up crossing any road, highway, or street, and you may have to do this training before you get your dog used to the crowded store.

Before attempting to make any crossing, first come to a halt, look both directions, and when traffic is clear, give the Heel command and cross over. Always take plenty of time to look over the situation. When moving vehicles have passed, take time to praise your dog, and he will learn that this is what you were waiting for.

It must be quite evident by now that we've been trying hard to impress you with the importance of doing all your basic training *on lead*, regardless of what advanced training and distance control you may be aiming for. No matter what you do in this world, as the old adage goes, "If it's worth doing, it's worth doing well." And if you are going to build something sturdy and lasting, a firm foundation must come first. Otherwise it's subject to flaws and will collapse.

In any exercise you attempt *off lead*, make sure that the performance is tops *on lead*, then go through it a step at a time, gradually. Read your dog well, and he will let you know if you are going too fast or have skipped an important step along the way. Above all, keep the training sessions *fun* for both of you, and be pals to each other.

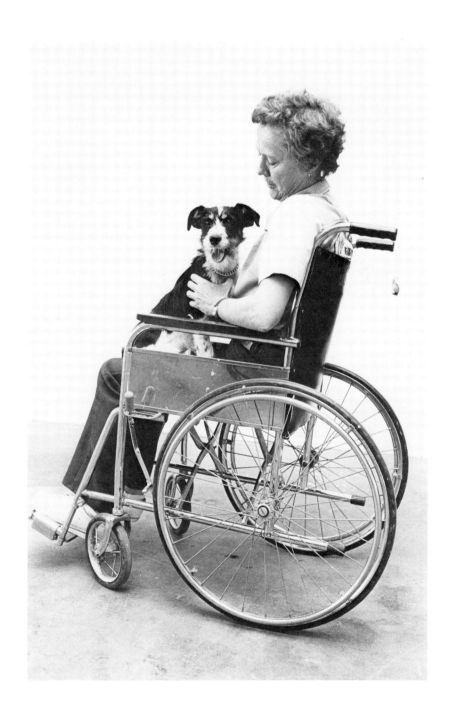

ABOUT THE AUTHOR

Margaret and Milo Pearsall began their career in obedience training in 1944. At that time most obedience was based on rigid techniques dictated by force, and the working relationship between dog and master reflected these negative methods. Not being comfortable with these methods Pearsalls developed their own way of training based on canine psychology and a positive approach. Seeing each new situation from the dog's point of view has enabled handlers to deal with each and every problem individually and has become accepted worldwide as one of the leading training methods. Many improvements in the techniques used today are due to Milo Pearsall's inventive imagination for developing training aids for the dogs, the handlers, and the teachers of training classes.

In 1963, Milo retired from his employment as an electrician to devote full time and attention to training classes. He and Margaret developed problem clinics throughout the country, held their own training classes, and upon request taught for other clubs. They were the first to incorporate five-day "instructor schools" to aid in further disseminating their theories and practices to the teachers of obedience classes. In addition, they have made several education films and did three thirteen-week training sessions via television in New York City.

Known internationally for their writing as well as their training techniques, Pearsalls have co-authored two previous training books, THE GUIDE TO SUCCESSFUL DOG TRAINING, by

Margaret and Milo, and DOG OBEDIENCE TRAINING, by Milo Pearsall and Charles G. Leedham. They have had articles published in the *American Kennel Gazette, Off Lead, Front and Finish,* and *Dogs,* which carried a continuing bi-monthly column which received a Certificate of Merit from the Dog Writers Association of America.

Margaret and Milo Pearsall reside in Rockledge, Florida, where they continue to be involved in training and pioneering in the field of dog training.

SUGGESTED READING

The Pearsall Guide to Successful Dog Training. Margaret E. Pearsall, Howell Book House, Inc., New York, NY.

Dog Obedience Training. Milo D. Pearsall & Charles Leedham, Publ. Charles Scribner's Sons, New York, NY.

The Complete Dog Book. Howell Book House, Inc., New York, NY. (AKC official breed standards)

The New Knowledge of Dog Behavior. Clarence Pfaffenberger, Howell Book House, Inc., New York, NY.

Why Does Your Dog Do That? Bergman, Howell Book House, Inc., New York, NY.

ADDRESS REFERENCES

The American Kennel Club, 51 Madison Avenue, New York, NY 10010

Handi-Dogs, Inc., P.O. Box 12563, Tucson, AZ 85732

Hearing Dog, Inc., 5901 East 89th Avenue, Henderson, CO 80640

United States All American Dog Obedience Guild, Inc., P.O. Box 2576, El Cajon, CA 92024

Guide Dogs for the Blind, Box 1200, San Rafael, CA 94902

TRAINING AIDS

The authors can provide cassette training tapes for your practice sessions. They give directions and have a music background to help you keep a spirited rhythm as you train. Titles available include: Kindergarten Puppy Training, Beginning Obedience, Novice on Lead, Novice, Open, and Utility. Another cassette has different sounds to which you can introduce your dog while training. Write to the authors at 1025 Rockledge Drive, Apt. 201, Rockledge, Florida 32955 for further information.

Index

Photos were contributed by:
    The Authors
    John Gamber
    Hearing Dogs program
    Peter Chew
    Ray Jones
    Dr. H. Verbruggen
    Anne Williams

Diagrams and illustrations by:
    Kenneth Downs
    Mark Lowderman (hand signals)